GOWANS'

BIBLIOTHECA AMERICANA.

2

"Gather up the fragments that remain, that nothing be lost."
St. John.

"There is, perhaps, no nation in which it is so necessary, as in our own, to assemble, from time to time, the small tracts and fugitive pieces, which are occasionally published; for, besides the general subjects of enquiry, which are cultivated by us, in common with every other learned nation, our constitution in church and state naturally gives birth to a multitude of performances, which would either not have been written, or could not have been made publick in any other place."
S. Johnson.

NEW YORK:
WILLIAM GOWANS.

1860.

A

TWO YEARS JOURNAL

IN

NEW YORK,

AND PART OF ITS

TERRITORIES IN AMERICA.

BY CHARLES WOOLEY, A. M.

Wolley

A NEW EDITION WITH AN INTRODUCTION AND COPIOUS HISTORICAL NOTES

BY E. B. O'CALLAGHAN, M. D.,

CORRESPONDING MEMBER OF THE NEW YORK HISTORICAL SOCIETY.

Fir'd at the sound, my genius spreads her wing,
And flies where Britain courts the Western spring;
Where laws extend that scorn Arcadian pride,
And brighter streams than fam'd Hydaspis glide.
There all around the gentlest breezes stray,
There gentle music melts on ev'ry spray;
Creation's mildest charms are there combin'd;
Extremes are only in the master's mind!—Goldsmith.

For the Lord thy God bringeth thee into a good land, a land of brooks of water, of fountains, and depths that spring out of valleys and hills; a land of wheat and barley, and vines, and fig-trees, and pomegranates; a land of oil-olive, and honey; a land wherein thou shalt eat bread without scarceness, thou shalt not lack any thing in it; a land whose stones are iron, and out of whose hills thou mayest dig brass. When thou hast eaten and art full, then thou shalt bless the Lord thy God for the good land which he hath given thee. . . . . *Deuteronomy* 8: 7, 8.

NEW YORK:
WILLIAM GOWANS.

1860.

2

MUNSELL & ROWLAND, PRINTERS, ALBANY, N. Y.

DEDICATED

TO

THE MEMORY

OF

DE WITT CLINTON.

ADVERTISEMENT.

THE subscriber announces to the public, that he intends publishing a series of works, relating to the history, literature, biography, antiquities and curiosities of the Continent of America. To be entitled

GOWANS' BIBLIOTHECA AMERICANA.

The books to form this collection, will chiefly consist of reprints from old and scarce works, difficult to be procured in this country, and often also of very rare occurence in Europe : occasionally an original work will be introduced into the series, designed to throw light upon some obscure point of American history, or to elucidate the biography of some of the distinguished men of our land. Faithful reprints of every work published will be given to the public : nothing will be added, except in the way of notes, or introduction, which will be presented entirely distinct from the body of the work. They will be brought out in the best style, both as to the type, press work and paper, and in such a manner as to make them well worthy a place in any gentleman's library.

A part will appear about once in every six months, or oftener, if the public taste demand it; each part forming an entire work, either an original production, or a reprint of some valuable, and at the same time scarce tract. From eight to twelve parts will form a handsome octavo volume, which the publisher is well assured, will be esteemed entitled to a high rank in every collection of American history and literature.

Should reasonable encouragement be given, the whole collection may in the course of no long period of time become not less voluminous, and quite as valuable to the student in American history, as the celebrated Harleian Miscellany is now to the student and lover of British historical antiquities.

W. GOWANS, *Publisher.*

INTRODUCTION.

THE prevalent desire for authentic information on the early history of our country, encourages the publisher to endeavor to gratify such taste, by reprinting this curious and rare little Book, only three copies of which are, as far as he is informed, in these States. Though small, it throws light on the domestic manners and social habits of the people of the city of New York, in the latter part of the seventeenth century, not to be derived from larger and purely historical works.

Being curious to know the antecedents of its author, and having learned incidentally that he was a graduate of Cambridge, I addressed the authorities of that University and received, in answer, the following polite note, for which I beg to return my very sincere acknowledgments.

"TRINITY COLL. CAMBRIDGE.
"13 Oct. 1859.

"Dear Sir:

"The vice chancellor this day put into my hands your letter of the 24 Sept.

"I am sorry to say I can give no information as to the parentage of Charles Wolley. I have called upon the master of Emmanuel College and inspected the admission book in his custody. The information is very slight, it is as follows:

"'Ch. Wolley of Linc. admitted sizar 13 June, 1670.'

"The admission does not state whether he was born in the city of Lincoln or merely in the county: it does not mention Ch. W.'s father's name, or his place of education.

"The matriculation and degree books are in my custody:

"Charles Wolley was matriculated a sizar of Emm. Coll. on the 9 July, 1670.

Handwriting of B. A. degree.

"He took the degree of Bachelor of Arts in January, 1673-4, and his degree of Master of Arts in July, 1677.

Handwriting in M. A. degree.

"I send you tracings of his signature at both his degrees.

"Yours truly,

"JOSEPH ROMILLY

"E. B. O'Callaghan, Esq. (Registrary of the Univ^{ty})."

The year after he graduated Mr. WOLLEY came to New York. At the period referred to in his Journal, the province is described as "poore, unsettled and almost without trade;" the city was, "small in size and scanty in population; its buildings mostly wood; some few of stone and brick; 10 or 15 ships, of about 100 tons burthen each, frequented the port in a year; four of these being New York built." The annual imports were valued at £50,000, or $250,000; a trader worth $2500 to $5000 was "accompted a good substantial merchant; a planter whose moveables were valued at half that sum was esteemed rich. Ministers were scarce and Religions many." * The Church of England; the Reformed Dutch church; French Calvinists; Lutherans;

* N. Y. Col. Doc. iii., 261.

Roman Catholics; Quakers, both "singing and ranting;" Sabatarians and Anti-sabatarians; Anabaptists; Independents and Jews, all were represented. In short some of all sorts of opinions, and some of none at all, helped in those, as in these, days to compose the heterogeneous population of the metropolis.

Fort James was "seated upon a point of the towne, on a plot of ground containing about two acres, between Hudson River and ye Sound; it was a square with stone walls, four bastions almost regular, and in it 46 gunns mounted, and stores for service accordingly." * The "great house" had been covered with Dutch tiles; but these were removed and the roof covered with shingles, "by reason the Tyles were usually broken when the gunns were fired." An hospital, or officers' quarters, stood in the vicinity, between Stone and Bridge streets.

The garrison of the Fort consisted of

1 Captain (gov. Andros,) whose pay was 8s. stg. per day.

2 Lieuts. { Anthy Brockholes / Christopher Bellop } pay 4s. per day.

1 Ensign (Cæsar Knapton) pay 3s.

3 Sergeants @ 1s. 6 a day; 4 Corporals and 2 drummers @ 1s. a day; 100 privates @ 8d. per day; 1 master gunner @ 2s.; 4 matrosses @ 1s.; 1 Chirurgeon @ 2s.; 1 Storekeeper @ 2s. and "A Chaplaine" @ 6s. per day.

The "Chaplaine" here referred to was the Rev. CHARLES WOLLEY; his salary amounted to £121. 6s. 8d sterling, or about $600 a year. †

From his Journal we are led to conclude that he was a gentleman of learning and observation; social of habit and charitable in feeling. On his departure from this

* N. Y. Col. Doc. iii., 260. † Ibid, 220.

country, Sir Edmund Andros bore testimony to his proper deportment whilst here, in the following words:

"A Certificate to Mr. Charles Wolley to goe for England in the Hopewell.

"S[r] Edmund Andros Kn[t] &c. Whereas Mr. Charles Wolley (a Minister of the church of England) came over into these parts in the Month of August 1678 and hath officiated accordingly as Chaplaine under his Royall Highnesse during the time of his abode here, Now upon Applicacon for leave to returne for England in order to some promocōn in the church to which hee is presented, hee having liberty to proceede on his voyage. These are to certify the above and that the s[d] Mr. Wolley hath in his place comported himself unblameable in his Life and conversacōn. In Testimony whereof I have hereunto sett my hand and Seale of the province in New York this 15th day of July in the 32th yeare of his Matyes Raigne. Annoq Dominj 1680.

"Examined by mee M. N. Secr."*

Mr. Wolley returned to England in a ship commanded by George Heathcote, a Quaker, some particulars of whom will be found in Note 47, at the end of this volume. He took with him as curiosities, "a Grey squirrel, a Parrot, and a Raccoon," and if any desire be felt respecting the subsequent fortunes of these favorites, we are pleased to be able to say, that the same will be found fully satisfied on referring to the pages of the Journal.

We next find our author at Alford in Lincolnshire. Hoping to learn something further of his history, I wrote to the Rector of that church, who in return was so obliging as to take a great deal of trouble to obtain the requisite informa-

* N. Y. Gen. Entries, xxxii: 93.

tion, and communicated the result in the following letter:

"ALFORD VICARAGE
"Lincolnshire,
"September 17, 1859.

"Dear Sir:

"It would have given me great pleasure could I have assisted you in your enquiries respecting the Rev. CHARLES WOLLEY, but I am afraid I shall not be able to do so. As our registers at Alford begin within five years of the oldest in England I thought until your enquiry came to me that this parish might hold its head high in such lore. But upon searching them I found a great gap including the whole time you are enquiring about and extending from 1657 to 1732. I immediately wrote off to an American gentleman (one of the Hutchinson family) who searched them last year; and this morning his answer arrived but threw no light upon the missing portion. In the mean time I enquired of the old people who might be supposed familiar with traditionary names but met with no success.

"One more source is open to me, the old parochial (not ecclesiastical) books which I will examine before I close this. If this fails me I see not in what way I can be of service.

"I am Dear Sir
"Yours very truly,
"GEORGE JEANS.

"E. B. O'Callaghan, Esq[r].

"P. S. Sept. 21. The parish books begin in 1701, but there is no mention of the name. There is just a possibility it may occur in the records of the Governors of the Grammar School, which I will examine.

"Sept. 29. I regret to say I have examined the archives of the Governors of the Grammar School and cannot find the name through all the years you gave me.

G. J."

Still unwilling to abandon my search until all probable sources of information had been exhausted, I applied to the Lord Bishop of Lincoln, to whose diocese, it appeared by the admission book of Emmanuel College, Mr. Wolley belonged, requesting that I might be furnished by his Lordship's orders, with transcripts of any data the records of the diocese might supply on the subject of my enquiry. The following is an extract from the answer to that application:

"The Palace, Lincoln,
"Jan'y 19, 1860.

"Dear Sir:

"I have had the Books and Records of this Registry searched, but I have been unable to find even the Name of the Rev. Chas. Wolley, in this Diocese, and am strongly inclined to think that he never held a Benefice in it, otherwise the Register Books would shew it. From your observation, that he was removed "for his unprofitableness," I feel quite sure it was not any Benefice; no beneficed Clergyman could be removed from his Benefice on any such ground, nor a Curate either, if he objected and had not committed any crime. * * * * * * *
Of course you will understand that we have found no Record of his Ordination either, and therefore concluded it is a mistake altogether. He might be employed temporarily as a Curate at Alford, without being licensed, and then no record of it would be made. * * * * *

"I am Dear Sir
"Yours faithfully,
"William Moss."

"E. B. O'Callaghan, Esqr.

The close of Mr. WOLLEY'S career is thus shrouded in obscurity. His ministry appears by his own acknowledgment, not to have abounded in fruit; for, apologizing both for publishing, and for having delayed the publication of, his Journal, he says, that he was "taken off, from the proper studies and offices of his Function, for his unprofitableness;" and therefore concluded, when he could not do "what he ought," to do "what he could," and accordingly published this Journal.

It is evident, from various passages in these Reminiscences, that his sojourn in this country left a pleasing impression on Mr. WOLLEY'S mind. "New York," he says, "is a place of as sweet and agreeable air as ever I breathed in, and the inhabitants, both English and Dutch, very civil and courteous, as I may speak by experience, amongst whom I have often wished myself and my family."

I have endeavored to ascertain whether he carried out this wish and returned to this country. The name is found in our archives, posterior to the original publication of this Journal;* and Mr. Valentine states that a Charles Wooley was admitted a freeman of New York in 1702.† Whether or not, this was the former Chaplain of Fort James and Sojourner at Alford, I must leave to others to determine.

With a view to throw additional light on some passages of the Text, and further to illustrate the Men and Manners of Days which have long passed away, and all trace whereof is buried in ancient MSS. and dust-covered Tomes, Notes, historical and biographical, have been added to the Journal. In the preparation of these, every care has been taken to consult the best authorities within reach, and to

*N. Y. Doc. Hist., i., 622; N. Y. Col. Doc., iv: 934.

† Valentine's Hist. of the City of New York, 377.

state the authority consulted, in order that every one may have the means of reëxamining the points selected for illustration, if he feel so inclined. It is to be hoped that the pains and labor thus bestowed, will prove of profit to others and merit general approbation.

A two Years
JOURNAL
IN
New-York:
And part of its
TERRITORIES
IN
AMERICA.

By *C. W.* A. M.

LONDON,

Printed for *John Wyat*, at the *Rose* in St. *Paul's* Church-Yard: and *Eben Tracy*, at the three *Bibles* on *London-Bridge*. MDCCI.

TO THE READER.

The materials of this Journal have laid by me several years expecting that some Landlooper or other in those parts would have done it more methodically, but neither hearing nor reading of any such as yet, and I being taken off from the proper Studies and Offices of my Function, for my unprofitableness, I concluded, that when I could not do what I ought, I ought to do what I could, which I shall further endeavour in a second Part: in the mean while, adieu.

A

TWO YEARS JOURNAL

IN

NEW YORK, &C.

In the year 1678, May the 27, we set sail from old England for New-York in America, in the Merchants Ship called the Blossom, Richard Martain of New-England Master. (See Note 1.) We had on board Sir Edmund Andros, (see Note 2.) Governor of New-York, Merchants and Factors, Mr. William Pinhorne, (see Notc 3,) Mr. James Graham, (see Note 4,) Mr. John White, Mr. John West (see Note 5,) and others; the 7th of August following we arriv'd safe at New-York.

The City of New-York, by Dr. Heylin (see Note 6,) and other Cosmographers, is call'd New-Amsterdam, and the Country New-Netherlands, being first inhabited by a Colony of Dutch; but as first discover'd by the English it was claim'd to the Crown of England by Colonel Nichols, in the year 1665, (see Note 7,) then sent over Governor; to whom it was surrendred by the Dutch upon Articles; it being a fundamental Point consented unto by all Nations, That the first discovery of a Country inhabited by Infidels, gives a right and Dominion of that Country to the Prince in whose Service and Employment the discoverers were sent; thus the Spaniard claims the West-Indies; the Portugals Brasile; and thus the English those Northern parts of America; (see Note 8,) for Sebastian Cabot (see Note 9,) employed by K. Hen. 7th, was the first discoverer of those parts, and in his name took Possession, which his Royal Successors have held and continu'd ever since: Therefore they are of the Crown of England, and as such they are accounted by that excellent Lawyer Sir John Vaughan: (see Note 10,) So this particular Province being granted to his then Royal-Highness the D. of York, by Letters Patents from King Charles the II. was from his title and Propriety call'd New-York.

The Fort and Garrison of this place lieth in the degree of 40th and 20 minutes of northern Latitude, (see Note 11,) as was observ'd and taken by Mr. Andrew Norwood, Son of the Famous Mathematician of that name, (see Note 12,) and by Mr. Philip Wells, (see Note 13,) and Van Cortland Junior, Robert Rider and Jacobus Stephens, the seventh of July 1679, with whom I was well acquainted, and at that time present with them.

The Temperature of the Climate

By the Latitude above observ'd, New-York lieth 10 Degrees more to the Southward than Old England; by which difference according to Philosophy it should be the hotter Climate, but on the contrary, to speak feelingly, I found it in the Winter Season rather colder for the most part: the reason of which may be the same with that which

Sir Henry Wotton (see Note 14,) gives for the coldness of Venice, as he observ'd from the experience of fourteen years Embassie, viz. Though Venice be seated in the very middle point, between the Equinoctial and the northern Pole, at 45 degrees precisely, or there abouts, of Latitude, yet their winters are for the most part sharper than ours in England, though about six degrees less of Elevation, which he imputed to its vicinity or nigh Situation to the chilly tops of the Alps, for Winds as well as Waters are tainted and infected in their passage. New-York in like manner is adjacent to and almost encompass'd with an hilly, woody Country, full of Lakes and great Vallies, which receptacles are the Nurseries, Forges and Bellows of the Air, which they first suck in and contract, then discharge and ventilate with a fiercer dilatation. The huge lake of Canada, which lies to the northward of New-York, is supposed to be the most probable place for dispersing the cold Northwest-winds which alter the nature of this Climate, insomuch that a thick winter Coat there is commonly called a North-western: So that the Consequence which Men make in common discourse from the Degree of a place to the temper of it, is indeed very deceivable, without a due regard to other circumstances; for as I have read in the Philosophical Transactions, the order of the seasons of the year is quite inverted under the torrid Zone, for whereas it should be then Summer when the Sun is near, and Winter when the Sun is farther of; under the torrid Zone it's never less hot than when the Sun is nearest; nor more hot than when the Sun is farthest off; so that to the people who live between the Equinoctial and the Tropicks, Summer begins about Christmas, and their Winter about St. John's day, the reason whereof is that when the Sun is directly over their heads, it raises abundance of Vapours, and draws them so high that they are presently converted into water by the coldness of the Air; whence it comes to pass that then it rains continually, which does repress the Air; but when the Sun is farther off there falls no more Rain, and so the heat becomes insupportable; but besides these Observations and Philosophical Solutions, give me leave to offer one Consideration to the Inhabitants of the Northern parts of England, viz. Whether they have not taken notice for the several years past of some alteration in the Seasons of the year; that the Winters have been earlier, colder and longer, and the Summers shorter than formerly within their own memories; for which I think I may appeal to the Gardeners. Especially as to the fruit of the Vine, no Grapes having come to their maturity or perfection in the same Gardens they used to do: Now to what reasons shall we impute these, shall we say in the words of that Scribe of the Law, Esdras, The world hath lost his youth, and the times begin to wax old, for look how much the world shall be weaker through age? Or shall we apologize with Dr. Hakewell, (see Note 15,) in his Power and Providence in the Government of the World? For my part I humbly submit to the

Virtuoso's of Natural and Divine Philosophy; rather than embarass and envelop my self in prying within the Curtains of the Primitive Chaos, or the Womb of the Creation, or the dark Orb of Futurities.

Of the Air.

It's a Climate of a Sweet and wholesome breath, free from those annoyances which are commonly ascribed by Naturalists for the insalubrity of any Country, viz. South or South-east Winds, many stagnant Waters, lowness of shoars, inconstancy of Weather, and the excessive heat of the Summer; the extremity of which is gently refresh'd, fann'd and allay'd by constant breezes from the Sea; it does not welcome its Guests and Strangers with the seasoning distempers of Fevers and Fluxes, like Virginia, Maryland, and other Plantations, nature kindly drains and purgeth it by Fontanels and Issues of running waters in its irriguous Valleys, and shelters it with the umbrella's of all sorts of Trees from pernicious Lakes; which Trees and Plants do undoubtedly, tho' insensibly suck in and digest into their own growth and composition, those subterraneous Particles and Exhalations, which otherwise wou'd be attracted by the heat of the Sun and so become matter for infectious Clouds and malign Atmospheres, and tho we cannot rely upon these causes as permanent and continuing, for the longer and the more any Country is peopled, the more unhealthful it may prove, by reason of Jaques, Dunghills and other excrementitious stagnations, which offend and annoy the bodies of Men, by incorporating with, and infecting the circumambient Air, but these inconveniencies can scarce be suppos'd to happen within our age, for the very settling and inhabiting a new Country, which is commonly done by destroying its Wood, and that by Fire (as in those parts I describe) does help to purifie and refine the Air; an experiment and remedy formerly us'd in Greece and other Nations, in the time of Plague or any common infection. To conclude this Chapter, I my self, a person seemingly of a weakly Stamen and a valetudinary Constitution, was not in the least indispos'd in that Climate, during my residence there, the space of three years: This account and description of the place, I recommend as a fair encouragement, to all who are inclined to Travel; to which I shall subjoin other inviting Advantages and Curiosities in their proper places.

Of the Inhabitants. And first of the Indians or Natives.

There are a clan of highflown Religionists, who stile the Indians the Populus Terræ, and look upon them as a reprobate despicable sort of creatures: But making the allowances for their invincible ignorance, as to a reveal'd Education, I should rather call them the Terræ filii: For otherwise I see no difference betwixt them and the rest of the Noble Animals. They are stately and well proportioned in Symmetry through the whole Oeconomy of their bodies, so that I cannot say I observed any natural deformity in any of them; which probably may be owing to their way of nurturing their new born Infants: which is thus, as soon as a Woman is delivered, she retires into the Wood for a burden or bundle of sticks, which she takes upon her back to strengthen her; the Children they Swaddle upon a Board, which they hang about their heads, and so carry them for a year together, or till they can go, this I had confirm'd to me, by my friend Mr. William Asfordby, (see Note 16,) who lived in those parts sixteen years, and had for his Neighbour one Harman the Indian in Marble-Town, in the County of Ulster, formerly called Sopus, (see Note 17,) in the Province of New-York, whose Squaw or Wife us'd this way to her self and Children: In nursing their Children, the Mother abhors that unnatural and Costly Pride of suckling them with other Breasts, whilst her own are sufficient for that affectionate service; their hardiness and facility in bringing forth is generally such as neither requires the nice attendance of Nursekeepers, nor the art of a dextrous Lucina, being more like the Hebrew Women than the native Ægyptians, delivered before the Midwife can come to them; like that Irish Woman of whom Dr. Harvy (see Note 18,) de generatione Animalium, Cap. de partu, Page 276, reports from the mouth of the Lord Carew, Earl of Totness and Lord President of Munster, (see Note 19,) who though big with Child accompanied her Husband in the Camp, marching from place to place, but by reason of a sudden flood which hindered their Armies march for one hour, the Woman's pains coming upon her, she withdrew her-self to a thicket of Shrubs, and there alone brought forth Twins, both which she brought down to the River and wash'd both herself and them, wrapping them up in a course and Irish Mantle, marches with them at her back, the same day barefoot and barelegged twelve Miles, without any prejudice to herself or them. The next day after, the Lord Deputy Montjoy, (see Note 20,) who at that time commanded the Army against the Spaniard, who had besieged Kinsale, with the Lord Carew, stood God-fathers for the Children; but I cannot say of them as it is related of the Queen of Navarre, Mother to Henry of France, called the Great, who sung a French Song in the time of his Birth, seeming to show other Women, that it is possible to be brought to bed without crying out.

As to their Stature, most of them are between five or six foot high, straight bodied, strongly composed, in complexion perfect Adamites; of a clayish colour, the Hair of their Heads generally black, lank and long, hanging down. And I have been several times amongst them, and could never observe any one shap'd either in redundance or defect, deformed or mishapen. They preserve their Skins smooth by anointing them with the Oyl of Fishes, the fat of Eagles, and the grease of Rackoons, which they hold in the Summer the best Antidote to keep their skins from blistering by the scorching Sun, their best Armour against the Musketto's; the surest expeller of the hairy Excrement, and stopper of the Pores of their Bodies against the Winter's cold, their Hair being naturally black, they make it more so, by oyling, dying and dayly dressing, yet though they be very curious about the Hair of their Heads, yet they will not endure any upon their Chins, where it no sooner grows but they take it out by the Roots, counting it a spurious and opprobrious excrement: Insomuch, that the Aberginians (see Note 21,) or Northern Indians in New-England, call him an English-man's Bastard, that hath but the appearance of a Beard; so that I leave it to the other Sex:

Judicat ex mento non mente puella maritum.

Of their Apparel.

Notwithstanding the heat of parching Summers, and the searching cold of piercing Winters, and the tempestuous dashings of driving Rains, their ordinary habit is a pair of Indian Breeches, like Adam's Apron to cover that which modesty commands to be hid, which is a piece of Cloth about a yard and a half long, put between their groins, tied with a Snake's Skin about their middle, and hanging down with a flap before, many of them wear skins about them in fashion of an Irish Mantle and of these some be Bears Skins and Rackoon Skins sewed or skuered together; but of late years, since they trade with the English and Dutch, they wear a sort of Blanket, which our

Merchants call Duffles, which is their Coat by day and covering by night, I have heard of some reasons given why they will not conform to our English Apparel, viz. because their Women cannot wash them when they are soiled, and their means will not reach to buy new, when they have done with their old, therefore they had rather go as they do, than be lowsie and make their bodies more tender by a new acquired habit, but they might be easily divested of these reasons, if they were brought to live in Houses and fix'd Habitations, as I shall shew hereafter. Though in their habit they seem to be careless and indifferent, yet they have an instinct of natural Pride, which appears in their circumstantial Ornaments, many of them wearing Pendants at their Ears, and Porcupine-quills through their Noses, impressing upon several parts of their bodies Portraictures of Beasts and Birds, so that were I to draw their Effigies it should be after the pattern of the Ancient Britains, called Picts from painting, and Britains from a word of their own Language, Breeth, Painting or Staining, as Isidore writes, with whom Mr. Cambden (see Note 22,) concurs; though Dr. Skinner (see Note 23,) in his Etymologicon Onomasticon, a Bri. honor & Tain fluvius, Insula fluviis nobilis: But to leave these Authors in their own crictical ingenuity, I shall conclude this Chapter with a general Sentiment of such Customs that by these variety of Pictures depourtraicted in their Bodies; they are either ambitious to illustrate and set off their natural Symmetry, or to blazon their

Heraldy, which a certain Author calls Macculoso Nobilitas: Or else to render them terrible and formidable to all Strangers: or if we may conjecture out of that Rabbinical Critick the Oxford Gregory upon Cain's Thau, that according to the natural Magicians and Cabbalists, Adam and the rest of mankind in his right, had marks imprinted upon them by the finger of God, which marks were, pachad and chesed; the first to keep the Beasts in awe of Men; the latter to keep Men in love one with another. Whether there be any remains of a traditional imitation in the Indian World or not, I leave that and other conjectures to the Readers diversion.

Of their Traffick, Money, and Diet.

They live principally by Hunting, Fishing and Fowling. Before the Christians especially the Dutch came amongst them they were very dexterous Artists at their Bows, insomuch I have heard it affirm'd that a Boy of seven years old would shoot a Bird flying: and since they have learn'd the use of Guns, they prove better marksmen than others, and more dangerous too (as appear'd in the Indian War with New-England.) The Skins of all their Beasts, as Bears, Bevers, Rackoons, Foxes, Otters; Musquashes, Skunks, Deer and Wolves, they bring upon their backs to New-York, and other places of Trade, which they barter and exchange for Duffles or Guns, but too often for Rum, Brandy and other strong Liquors, of which they are so intemperate lovers, that after they have once tasted, they will never forbear, till they are inflamed and enraged, even to that degree, that I have seen Men and their Wives Billingsgate it, through the Streets of New-York, as if they were metamorphosed into the nature of those beasts whose Skins they bartered: It were seriously to be wished that the Christians would be more sparing in the sale of that Liquor, which works such dismal effects upon those who are for gratifying their sensual Appetites: Being unacquainted with the comforts of Christian Temperance, and the elevated Doctrine of Self-denial and Mortification. They had better take to their primitive Beverage of water, which some Vertuoso's tell us breed no Worms in the Belly nor Maggots in the Brain.

Their Money is called Wampam and Sea-want, made of a kind of Cockle or Periwinkle-shell, of which there is scarce any, but at Oyster-Bay. They take the black out of the middle of the shell which they value as their Gold; they make their White Wampam or Silver of a kind of a Horn, which is beyond Oyster-bay: The meat within this horny fish is very good. They fashion both sorts like beads, and String them into several lengths, but the most usual measure is a Fathom; for when they make any considerable bargain, they usually say so many Fathom; So many black or so many white Wampams make a farthing, a penny, and so on: which Wampam or Indian Money we valued above the Spanish or English

Silver in any Payments, because of trading with the Indians in their own Coin. (See Note 24.) The price of Indian Commodities as sold by the Christian Merchants is as followeth.

		s.	d.	
Bevers	—00—	10—	3	a Pound.
The Lapps	—00—	07—	6	
Minks	—00—	05—	0	
Grey Foxes	—00—	03—	0	
Otters	—00—	08—	0	
Rackoons	—00—	01—	5	

Bever is fifteen pence a Skin Custom at New-York, four pence at London; three pence a Skin Freight, which is after the rate of fifteen Pound a Tun.

The value of other Skins, a Deer Skin 00—00—6 a p. A good Bear Skin will give 00—07—0. A black Bever-skin is worth a Bever and a half of another colour. A black Otter's-skin, if very good, is worth Twenty Shillings. A Fisher's-skin three shillings. A Cat's-skin half a Crown. A Wolf's-skin three shillings. A Musquash or a Muskrat's-skin six shillings and ten pence. An Oxe-hide three pence a pound wet and six pence dry. Rum in Barbados ten pence a Gallon. Molossus three pence a pound, and fifty shillings a barrel in winter, that being the dearest season. Sugar in Barbados twelve shillings the hundred which contains a hundred and twelve pounds; which at New-York yields thirty shillings the bare hundred. In Barbados (new Negro's i. e. such as cannot speak English) are bought for twelve or fourteen pound a head, but if they can speak English sixteen or seventeen pound; and at New-York, if they are grown Men, they give thirty five and thirty or forty Pound a head; (see Note 25,) where by the by let me observe that the Indians look upon these Negroes or Blacks as an anomalous Issue, meer Edomites, hewers of Wood and drawers of Water.

The Price of Provisions: Long Island Wheat three shillings a Skipple (a Skipple being three parts of a Bushel) Sopus Wheat half a Crown a Skipple, Sopus Pease half a Crown a Skipple; Indian Corn Flower fifteen shillings a hundred, Bread 18 a hundred. To Barbados 50s. a Tun freight, 4 Hogsheads to a Tun; Pork 3l. the barrel, which contains two hundred and 40 pounds, i. e. 3d. the pound; Beef 30s. the barrel; Butter 6d. a Pound: amongst Provisions I may reckon Tobacco, of which they are obstinate and incessant Smoakers, both Indians and Dutch, especially the latter, whose Diet especially of the boorish sort, being Sallets and Bacon, and very often picked buttermilk, require the use of that herb to keep their phlegm from coagulating and curdling. I once saw a pretty instance relating to the power of Tobacco, in two Dutchmen riding a race with short campaigne Pipes in their mouths, one of which being hurl'd from his Steed, as soon as he gathered himself up again, whip'd to his Pipe, and fell a sucking and drawing, regarding neither his Horse nor Fall, as if the prize consisted in getting that heat which came from his beloved smoke:

They never burn their Pipes, but as soon as they are out put them into their Pockets, and now and then wash them. The Indians originally made Pipes of Flint, and have some Pipes of Steel; they take the leaves of Tobacco and rub them betwixt their hands, and so smoke it; Tobacco is two pence halfpenny a pound, a merchantable Hogshead contains four hundred pound neat, i. e. without the Cask. A Dutch pound contains eighteen ounces. Pipe staves are fifty shillings or three pound a thousand, they are sent from New-York to the Madera Islands and Barbados, the best is made of White Oak. Their best Liquors are Fiall, Passado, and Madera Wines, the former are sweetish, the latter a palish Claret, very spritely and generous, two shillings a Bottle; their best Ale is made of Wheat Malt, brought from Sopus and Albany about threescore Miles from New-York by water; Syder twelve shillings the barrel; their quaffing liquors are Rum-Punch and Brandy-punch, not compounded and adulterated as in England, but pure water and pure Nants.

The Indians Diet.

What they liv'd upon originally is hard to determine, unless we recur to St. John Baptist's extemporary Diet in the Wilderness, for they may be properly called *ἱλόβιοι*, i. e. Inhabitants of the Wood, so may be supposed to have had their *victus parabilis*, food that wanted no dressing; but stories of the first times being meerly conjectural,

I shall only speak what I wrote down from the best information. They have a tradition that their Corn was at first dropt out of the mouth of a Crow from the Skies; just as Adam de Marisco (see Note 26,) was wont to call the Law of Nature Helias's Crow, something flying from Heaven with Provisions for our needs. They dig their ground with a Flint, called in their Language tom-a-hea-kan, (see Note 27,) and so put five or six grains into a hole the latter end of April or beginning of May, their Harvest is in October, their Corn grows like clusters of Grapes, which they pluck or break off with their hands, and lay it up to dry in a thin place, like unto our Cribs made of reed; when its well dryed they parch it, as we sprekle Beans and Pease, which is both a pleasant and a hearty food, and of a prodigious encrease, even a hundred fold, which is suppos'd as the highest degree of fruitfulness, which often reminded me of the Marquess of Worcester's (see Note 28,) Apophthegm of Christ's Miracle of five Loves and two Fishes, viz. that as few grains of Corn as will make five Loves being sowed in the earth will multiply and increase to such advantage as will feed 5000 with Bread, and two Fishes will bring forth so many fishes as will suffice so many mouths, and because such are so ordinary amongst us every day, we take no notice of them: this Indian Corn is their constant Viaticum in their travels and War. Their Squaws or Wives and Female Sex manage their Harvest, whilest the Men Hunt and Fish, and Fowl; of which they bring all varieties to New-York, and that so cheap that I remember a Venison bought for three shillings; their Rivers are plentifully furnish'd with fish, as Place, Pearch, Trouts, Eels, Bass and Sheepshead, the two last are delicate Fish: They have great store of wild-fowl, as Turkeys, Heath-hens, Quails, Partridges, Pigeons, Cranes, Geese, Brants, Ducks, Widgeon, Teal and divers others: And besides their natural Diet, they will eat freely with the Christians, as I observed once when we were at dinner at the Governor's Table, a Sackamaker or King came in with several of his Attendants, and upon invitation sat round upon the Floor (which is their usual posture) and ate of such Meat as was sent from the Table: amongst themselves when they are very hungry they will eat their Dogs, which are but young Wolves stolen from their damms, several of which I have seen following them, as our Dogs here, but they won't eat of our Dogs because they say we feed them with salt meat, which none or but few of the Indians love, for they had none before the Christians came: so unacquainted were they with Acids: They are of opinion that when they have ill success in their hunting, fishing, &c. their Menitto is the cause of it, therefore when they have good success they throw their fat into the fire as a Sacrifice ingeminating Kenah Menitto, i. e. I thank you Menitto; their Kin-tau Kauns, (see Note 29,) or time of sacrificing is at the beginning of winter, because then all things are fat, where a great many Sacka-makers or

Kings meet together, and Feast; every Nation or Tribe has its Ka-kin-do-wet, (see Note 30,) or Minister, and every Sacka-maker gives his Ka-kin-do-wet 12 fathom of Wampam mixt, and all that are able at that time throw down Wampam upon the ground for the Poor and Fatherless, of whom they have a great many. Now I am speaking of fishing and fowling it may not be improper to add some thing about the art of catching Whales, which is thus, two Boats with six Men in each make a Company, viz. four Oars-men or Rowers; an Harpineer and a Steers-man; about Christmas is the season for Whaling, for then the Whales come from the North-east, Southerly, and continue till the latter end of March, and then they return again; about the Fin is the surest part for the Harpineer to strike: As soon as he is wounded, he makes all foam, with his rapid violent Course, so that if they be not very quick in clearing their main Warp to let him run upon the tow, which is a line fastned to the Harping-iron about 50 fathoms long, its a hundred to one he over-sets the Boat: As to the nature of a Whale, they copulate as Land-beasts, as is evident from the female Teats and Male's Yard, and that they Spawn as other Fishes is a vulgar error, Lam. 4. 3. even the Sea monsters draw out the breast they give suck to their young ones. For further its observable that their young Suckers come along with them their several courses. A Whale about 60 foot long having a thick and free Blubber may yield or make 40 or 50 barrels of Oyl, every Barrel containing 31 or 32 Gallons at 20s. a Barrel, if it hath a good large bone it may be half a Tun or a Thousand weight, which may give 25l. Sterling old England Money. A Dubartus is a Fish of the shape of a Whale, (see Note 31,) which have teeth where the Whale has Bone, there are some 30 or 40 foot long, they are call'd by some the Sea-Wolf, of them the Whales are afraid, and do many times run themselves ashore in flying from them, this is prov'd by the Whalers who have seen them seize upon them: the Blubber of the Whale will sometimes be half a yard thick or deep, if the Blubber be not fat and free, the Whale is call'd a Dry-skin; a Scrag-tail Whale is like another, only somewhat less, and his bone is not good, for it will not split, and it is of a mixt colour, their Blubber is as good for the quantity as others: I never heard of any Spermaceti Whales, either catch'd or driven upon these Shores, which Sperma as they call it (in the Bahama Islands) lies all over the body of these Whales, they have divers Teeth which may be about as big as a Man's wrist, which the ordinary Whales have not, they are very strong, fierce and swift, inlaid with Sinews all over their bodies. But to leave this Leviathan to his pastime in the deep, let us go a shore, and speak something of the nature of a Beaver, in hunting of which the Indians take great pains and pleasure; the Beaver hath two sorts of Hair, one short soft and fine to protect him from the cold, the other long and thick, to receive the dirt and mire, in which they are often busie and employed, and to hinder it from spoiling the skin ; his teeth are of a peculiar contexture, fit to cut boughs and sticks, with which they build themselves houses, and lodgings of several stories and rooms, to breed their young ones in : for which purpose nature hath also furnish'd them with such forefeet as exactly resemble the feet of a Monkey, or the hands of a Man : their hind-feet proper for swimming, being like those of a Duck or Goose : As to the Castoreum or parts conceived to be bitten away to escape the Hunter, is a vulgar conceit, more owing to Juvenal and other poetical fancies than to any traditional truth, or the Etymologies of some bad Gramarians, deriving *Castore a castrando,* whereas the proper Latin word is *fiber*, and *castor*, but borrowed from the Greek, so called *quasi* γα'ςιος, i. e. animal ventricosum, from his swaggy and prominent belly : the particular account of which is in Dr. Brown's (see Note 32,) Vulgar Errors : but to be short, the bladders containing the Castoreum are distinct from the Testicles or Stones, and are found in both Sexes ; with which when the Indians take any of them they anoint their Traps or Gins which they set for these Animals, to allure and draw them hither.

As to the nature of Bears, their bringing forth their young informous and unshapen, I wholly refer you to Doctor Brown's said Vulgar Errors : the substance of their legs is of a particular structure, of a thick fattish ligament, very good to eat, and so the Indians say of their body, which is often their diet ; when they hunt them, they commonly go two or three in company with Guns: for in case one shoot and miss the Bear will make towards them, so they shoot one after another to escape the danger and make their Game sure: But without Guns or any Weapon except a good Cudgel or Stick. I was one with others that have had very good diversion and sport with them, in an Orchard of Mr. John Robinson's of New-York; (see Note 33), where we follow'd a Bear from Tree to Tree, upon which he could swarm like a Cat; and when he was got to his resting place, perch'd upon a high branch, we dispatc'd a youth after him with a Club to an opposite bough, who knocking his Paws, he comes grumbling down backwards with a thump upon the ground, so we after him again: His descending backwards is a thing particularly remarkable: Of which I never read any account, nor know not to what defect in its structure to impute it: unless to the want of the *intestinum cœcum,* which is the fourth Gut from the Ventricle or Stomach, and first of the thick Guts, which by reason of its divers infolds and turnings seems to have no end, and for that reason perhaps called cœcum or blind Gut: which being thick may probably detain the meat in the belly, in a descending posture: but these conjectures I wholly submit to the anatomical faculty: The Indians seems to have a great value for these animals, both for their skins and carkase-sake, the one good meat, the other good barter: And I may infer the same from a present which my acquaintance, old Claus the Indian, made me of a couple of well grown Bears

Cubs, two or three days before I took Shiping for England, he thinking I would have brought them along with me, which present I accepted with a great deal of Ceremony (as we must every thing from their hands) and ordered my Negro boy about 12 years old to tye them under the Crib by my Horse, and so left them to any ones acceptance upon my going aboard: I brought over with me a Grey Squirrel, a Parret and a Rockoon, the first the Lady Sherard (see Note 34,) had some years at Stapleford, the second, I left at London; the last I brought along with me to Alford, where one Sunday in Prayer time some Boys giving it Nutts, it was choaked with a shell: It was by nature a very curious cleanly Creature, never eating any thing but first washed it with its forefeet very carefully: the Parot was a pratling familiar bird, and diverting company in my solitary intervals upon our Voyage home. As I was talking with it upon the Quarter Deck, by a sudden rowling of the Ship, down drops Pall overboard into the Sea and cry'd out amain poor Pall: The Ship being almost becalm'd, a kind Seaman threw out a Rope, and Pall seiz'd it with his Beak and came safe aboard again: This for my own diversion. As the Serpent was the most dangerous reptile in Paradise, so is the Rattle Snake in the Wilderness. It has its name from the configuration of its skin, which consists of several foldings which are all contracted *dum latet in herba*, whilst it lies on the grass, or at the root of some rotten Tree, from whence it often surprizes the unwary traveller, and in throwing himself at his legs: The dilating of these folds occasion a rattling. Wherever it penetrates or bites it certainly poysons: they are in their greatest vigour in July; but the all-wise Providence which hath furnish'd every Climate with antidotes proper for their distempers and annoyances, has afforded great plenty of Penny-royal or Ditany, whose leaves bruised are very hot and biting upon the Tongue, which being tied in a clift of a long stick, and held to the nose of a Rattle Snake, will soon kill it by the smell and scent thereof; the vertues of this Plant are so effectual, that we read by taking of it inwardly, or by outward application and by fume it will expell a dead Child. And the juice of it applied to wounds made by Sword, or the biting of venomous creatures is a present remedy: but besides this, I shall speak of another way of drawing out the poyson of these Creatures, which is by sucking of it out with their mouths, which one Indian will do for another, or for any Christian so poyson'd: A rare example of pure humanity, even equal to that of the Lady Elenor, the Wife of King Edward the first, who when her Husband had three wounds given him with the poysoned Knife of Anzazim the Saracen, two in the Arm and one near the Arm-pit, which by reason of the envenom'd blade were fear'd to be mortal, and when no Medicine could extract the poyson, his Lady did it with her Tongue, licking dayly while her Husband slept, his rankling wounds, whereby they perfectly clos'd, and yet her self receiv'd no harm, so sovereign a medicine is a good Tongue, beyond the attractive power of Cupping Glasses and Cauteries. It were to be wish'd that where Penny-royal or Dittany is scarce or unknown, that every Country family understood the vertue of Rue or Herb-a-grace, which is held as a preservative against infectious Diseases, and cures the biting of a mad Dog or other venom, which would be no invasion upon, or striving with the dispensatory of Pestal and Mortar, Still and Furnace; which legal faculties and professions being established and encourag'd by the wise constitutions of Governments, should not be interlop'd and undermin'd by persons of any other faculties, who are too apt to add temporal Pluralities to their spiritual Cures. Indeed it is a duty owing to human nature, to administer to and assist any one *in forma pauperis,* but to take a fee a reward or gratuity from a Naaman or a person able to employ the proper faculty, is to act the Gehazi, and not the Prophet Elisha; *Miles equis, piscator aquis,* an hammer for the Smith, an Homer for the School, let the Shooe-maker mind his Boot, and the Fisherman his Boat, the Divine his Sermon, and the Doctor his Salmon. This digression I hope will be taken as it's written with an impartial deference to both professions: for as we are taught from Jesus the Son of Sirach, to honor the physician for his skill, and the Apothecary for his confections, Ecclesiasticus chap. 38. 1. 8. so we are taught from a greater than he, to honor and revere the Doctors of souls, the holy Jesus the Son of God, for their Spiritual Cures and Dispensatories: But to return to the Indians, they have Doctors amongst them, whom they call Me-ta-ow, (see Note 35,) to whom every one gives something for there Cure, but if they die nothing at all, and indeed their skill in simples costs them nothing, their general remedy for all diseases is their sweating: Which is thus: when they find themselves any ways indisposed, they make a small Wigwam or House, nigh a River-side, out of which in the extremity of the Sweat they plunge themselves into the Water; about which I discoursed with one of their Me-ta-ows, and told him of the European way of Sweating in Beds, and rubbing our bodies with warm cloths: to which he answered he thought theirs the more effectual way: because the water does immediately stop all the passages (as he call'd the Pores) and at the same time wash off the excrementitious remainder of the Sweat, which he thought could not be so clearly done by friction or rubbing; which practice I leave to the consideration or rather diversion of the Physicians and their Balneo's: but this experiment prov'd Epidemical in Small-Pox, by hindering them from coming out. As to their way of living, it's very rudely and rovingly, shifting from place to place, according to their exigencies, and gains of fishing and fowling and hunting, never confining their rambling humors to any settled Mansions. Their Houses which they call Wigwams are as so many Tents or Booths covered with the barks of Trees, in the midst of which they have their fires, about which they sit in the day time, and lie in the nights; they are so Saturnine that they love extremes either to sit still or to be in robustous motions, spending their time in drowsie conferences, being naturally unenclin'd to any but lusory pastimes and exercises; their Diet in general is raw Flesh, Fish, Herbs, and Roots or such as the Elements produce without the concoction of the fire to prepare it for their Stomachs; so their Horses are of a hardy temperament, patient of hunger and cold, and in the sharp winter, when the ground is cover'd with Snow, nourish themselves with the barks of Trees, and such average and herbage as they can find at the bottom of the Snow: But now I am speaking of Horses, I never could be inform'd nor ever did see an Indian to have been on Horseback: Of which there are great ranges runing wild in the Woods, to which they pretend no right: but leave them to the Dutch and English Chevaliers to tame and manage; for which I often wondered there were not cheif Rangers, and a *Charta de Foresta* to regulate such Games. When they travel by water, they have small Boats, which they call Canoes, made of the barks of Trees, so very narrow, that two can neither sit nor stand a breast, and those they row with long paddles, and that so swiftly, that they'll skim away from a Boat with four Oars, I have taken a particular pleasure in plying these paddles, standing upright and steddy, which is their usual posture for dispatch: In which they bring Oysters and other fish for the Market: they are so light and portable that a Man and his Squaw will take them upon their Sholders and carry them by Land from one River to another, with a wonderful expedition; they will venture with them in a dangerous Current, even through Hell-gate it self, which lies in an arm of the Sea, about ten miles from New-York Eastward to New-England, as dangerous and as unaccountable as the Norway Whirl-pool or Maelstrom: in this Hell-gate which is a narrow passage, runneth a rapid violent Stream both upon Flood and Ebb; and in the middle lieth some Islands of Rocks, upon which the Current sets so violently, that it threatens present Shipwrack; and upon the Flood is a large whirlpool, which sends forth a continual hedious roaring; it is a place of great defence against an Enemy coming that way, which a small Fortification would absolutely prevent, by forcing them to come in at the west-end of Long-Island by Sandy-Hook, where Nutten-Island would force them within the command of the Fort of New-York, which is one of the strongest and best situated Garrisons in the North parts of America, and was never taken but once through the default of one Captain Manning, who in absence of the Governour suffered the Dutch to take it; for which he was condemned to an Exile to a small Island from his name, call'd Manning's Island, where I have been several times with the said Captain, whose entertainment was commonly a Bowl of Rum-Punch. (See Note 36.) In deep Snows the Indians with broad Shoos much in the shap of the round part of our Rackets which we use at Tennis: will travel without sinking in the least: at other times their common ordinary Shooes are parts of raw Beasts-skins tied about their feet: when they travel, for directing others who follow them, they lay sticks across, or leave some certain mark on Trees. Now I am speaking of the Indian Shooes, I cannot forbear acquainting the Reader that I seldom or never observ'd the Dutch Women wear any thing but Slippers at home and abroad, which often reminded me of what I read in Dr. Hamond (see Note 37,) upon the 6th of Ephesians, N. B. that the Ægyptian Virgins were not permitted to wear Shooes, i. e. not ready to go abroad: like the custom among the Hebrews, whose women were call'd ὀικοεις, *domi portæ* and οικȣρȣσαὶ home-setters and ὀικȣρικαὶ house bearers, the Heathen painted before the modest women's doors Venus sitting upon a Snail, *quæ domi porta vocatur*, called a House bearer, to teach them to stay at home, and to carry their Houses about with them. So the Virgins were called by the Hebrews *Gnalamoth, absconditæ*, hid, and the places of their abodes ϖαρθηνωναὶ, *cellæ Virginales*, Virgins Cells. Contrary to these are Whores Pro. 7. II. her feet abide not in her house, therefore the Chaldees call her *Niphcathhara* going abroad, and an Harlot the Daughter of an Harlot, *egredientem filiam egredientis*, a goer forth, the Daughter of a goer forth; and when Dinah went out to see the Daughters of the Land, and was ravish'd by Sichem: Simeon and Levi cry out, should he deal with our Sister as with an Harlot, which the Targum renders, *an sicut exeuntem foras:* They have another custom differing from other Nations. They feast freely and merrily at the Funeral of any Friend, to which I have been often invited and sometimes a Guest, a custom derived from the Gentiles to the latter Jews, according to which says Josephus of Archelaus, he mourned seven days for his Father, and made a sumptuous Funeral Feast for the multitude, and he adds that this custom was the impoverishing of many Families among the Jews, and that upon necessity, for if a Man omitted it, he was accounted no pious Man. The Dutch eat and drink very plentifully at these Feasts; but I do not remember any Musick or Minstrels, or *monumentarii choraulæ* mentioned by Apuleius, or any of the Musick mentioned by Ovid *de fastis.*

Cantabis mœstis tibia funeribus.

So that perhaps it may be in imitation of David's example, who as soon as his child was dead, wash'd and anointed himself and ate his bread as formerly, 2 Sam. 12. 20. In all these Feasts I observ'd they sit Men and Women intermixt, and not as our English do Women and Men by themselves apart. (See Note 38.)

Of the Indians Marriages and Burials.

When an Indian has a mind to a woman (asking the consent of Parents) he gives her so many Fathom of Wampam according to his ability, then his betrothed covers her face for the whole year before she is married, which put me in mind of Rebekah, who took a veil and covered her self when she met Isaac, Gen. 24. 65 which veil (saith *Tertullian de velandis virginibus*) was a token of her modesty and subjection. The Husband doth not lie with his Squaw or Wife, whilst the Child has done Sucking, which is commonly two years, for they say the Milk will not be good if they get Children so fast. They bury their friends sitting upon their heels as they usually sit, and they put into their graves with them a Kettle, a Bow and Arrows, and a Notas or Purse of Wampam; they fancy that after their death they go to the Southward, and so they take their necessaries along with them; or perhaps like the uncircumcis'd in Ezek. 32. 27. who went down to the Grave with Weapons of War, and laid their Swords under their heads, the ensigns of Valor and Honor: as tho they would carry their strength to the grave with them, contrary to that of the Apostle, it is sown a weak body, 1 Cor. 15. They mourn over their dead commonly two or three days before they bury them: they fence and stockado their graves about, visiting them once a year, dressing the weeds from them, many times they plant a certain Tree by their Graves which keeps green all the year: They all believe they shall live as they do now, and think they shall marry, but must not work as they do here; they hold their Soul or Spirit to be the breath of Man: They have a Tradition amongst them that about five hundred years agoe, a Man call'd (Wach que ow) came down from above, upon a Barrel's-head, let down by a Rope, and lived amongst them sixty years, who told them he came from an happy place, where there were many of their Nations; and so he left them. And they have another Tradition of one Meco Nish, who had lain as dead sixteen days, all which time he was unburied, because he had a little warmth about his breast, and after sixteen days he lived again, in which interval he told them he had been in a fine place where he saw all that had been dead. Such Traditions as these ought to be lookt upon by the Professors of Christianity, as the Epileptick half moon Doctrine of that grand Enthusiast Mahomet, beyond whose Tomb hanging in the air his Superstitious Arabians are not able to lift their minds to the Kingdom of Heaven: So that the Mahometans Tomb and the Indians Tub may stand upon the same bottom, as to their Credit and Tradition: and the Indians after their rising again to the Southward shall Marry, Eat and Drink, may plead as fair for them as the Mahometans earthly Paradise of Virgins with fairer and larger eyes than ever they beheld in this world, and such like sensual enjoyments, which its even a shame to mention: or the Jews worldly Messiah, who ought all to be the dayly objects of our Christian prayers and endeavours for their Conversion, that they may believe and obtain a better Resurrection, even the *Necumah* (see Note 39,) the day of Consolation, when we shall be so wonderfully changed as to be fit Companions for Angels, and reign with our Saviour in his Glory, who only hath the words of eternal life. In order to which I shall endeavour to offer some proposals in a Second Part, *de propaganda fide;* and so conclude this with some mixt occasional observations, with all due respects to some modern Criticks: Whether Adam or Eve sewed their fig-leave together with needle and thread is not my business to be so nice as *rem istam acu tangere:* But this I am well inform'd of, That the Indians, make thread of Nettles pill'd when full ripe, pure white and fine, and likewise another sort of brownish thread of a small weed almost like a Willow, which grows in the Wood, about three foot high, which is called Indian Hemp, of which they likewise make Ropes and bring them to sell, which wears as strong as our Hemp, only it wont endure wet so well, of this they make their Baggs, Purses or Sacks which they call Notas, which word signifies a Belly, (see Note 40,) and so they call any thing that's hollow to carry any thing. Their work is weaving with their fingers, they twist all their thread upon their Thighs, with the palm of their hands, they interweave their Porcupine quills into their baggs, their Needles they make of fishes or small beast bones, and before the Christians came amongst them, they had Needles of Wood, for which Nutwood was esteemed best, called *Um-be-re-makqua*, their Axes and Knives they made of white Flint-stones; and with a Flint they will cut down any tree as soon as a carpenter with a Hatchet, which experiment was tried of late years by one Mr. Crabb of Alford in Lincolnshire, for a considerable wager, who cut down a large Tree with a flint, handled the Indian way, with an unexpected art and quickness. They make their Candles of the same wood that the Masts of Ships are made of, which they call *Woss-ra-neck.* (See Note 41.) Thus far of the Indians, in this first part, which were part of my own personal observations, and other good informations from one Claus an Indian, otherwise called Nicholas by the English, but Claus by the Dutch, with whom I was much acquainted, and likewise from one Mr. John Edsal the constant Interpreter betwixt the Governor and the Indians, and all others upon all important affairs, who was my intimate acquaintance, and his Son my Scholar and Servant, whose own hand-writing is in many of my Memorial's: One thing I had almost forgot, i. e. when the Indians look one another's Heads they eat the Lice and say they are wholesome, never throwing any away or killing them: In a word as they have a great many manly instincts of nature, so I observed them very civil and respectful both in their behaviour and entertainment; I cannot say that ever I met any company of them, which I frequently did in my walks out of the Town, but they would bow both Head and Knee, saying here comes the *Sacka-maker's Kakin-do-wet*, i. e. the Governours Minister, whom I always saluted again with all due ceremony. They are faith-guides in the woods in times of Peace, and as dangerous enemies in times of War. Their way of fighting is upon Swamps, i. e. Bogs and Quagmires, in sculking Ambushes, beyond Trees and in Thickets, and never in a body. When they intend War they paint their faces black, but red is the sun-shine of Peace. There are several Nations which may be more properly called Tribes of Indians.

Rockoway upon the South of Jamaica upon Long-Island, the 1.

Sea-qua-ta-eg, to the South of Huntingdon, the 2.

Unckah-chau-ge, Brooke-haven, the 3.

Se-tauck, Seatauchet North, the 4.

Ocqua-baug, South-hold to the North, the 5.

Shin-na-cock, Southampton, the greatest Tribe, the 6.

Mun-tauck, to the Eastward of East-Hampton, the 7.

All these are Long-Island Indians. (See Note 42)

The Tribes which are Friends.

Top-paun, the greatest, which consists of an hundred and fifty fighting young Men. It's call'd the greatest because they have the greatest Sachim or Sacka-maker, i. e. King, whose name is Maimshee.

The Second is Ma-nissing, which lies westward from Top-paun, two days Journey; it consists of three hundred fighting Men, the Sacka-makers name is called Taum-ma-hau-Quauk.

The Third, Wee-quoss-cah-chau. i. e. Westchester Indians, which consists of seventy fighting Men, the Sacka-makers name is Wase-sa-kin-now.

The Fourth, Na-ussin, or Neversinks, a Tribe of very few, the Sacka-makers name is Onz-zeech.

May the lover of Souls bring these scattered desert people home to his own Flock.

To return from the Wilderness into New-York, a place of as sweet and agreeable air as ever I breathed in, and the Inhabitants, both English and Dutch very civil and courteous as I may speak by experience, amongst whom I have often wished my self and Family, to whose tables I was frequently invited, and always concluded with a generous bottle of Madera. I cannot say I observed any swearing or quarrelling, but what was easily reconciled and recanted by a mild rebuke, except once betwixt two Dutch Boors (whose usual oath is Sacrament) which abateing the abusive language, was no unpleasant Scene. As soon as they met (which was after they had alarm'd the neighbourhood) they seized each other's hair with their forefeet, and down they went to the Sod, their Vrows and Families crying out because they could not part them, which fray happening against my Chamber window, I called up one of my acquaintance, and ordered him to fetch a kit full of water and discharge it at them, which immediately cool'd their courage, and loosed their grapples: so we used to part our Mastiffs in England. In the same City of New-York where I was Minister to the English, there were two other Ministers or Domines as they were called there, the one a Lutheran a German or High-Dutch, the other a Calvinist an Hollander or Low-Dutchman, who behav'd themselves one towards another so shily and uncharitably as if

Luther and Calvin had bequeathed and entailed their virulent and bigotted Spirits upon them and their heirs forever They had not visited or spoken to each other with any respect for six years together before my being there, with whom I being much acquainted, I invited them both with their Vrows to a Supper one night unknown to each other, with an obligation, that they should not speak one word in Dutch, under the penalty of a Bottle of Medera, alledging I was so imperfect in that Language that we could not manage a sociable discourse, so accordingly they came, and at the first interview they stood so appaled as if the Ghosts of Luther and Calvin had suffered a transmigration, but the amaze soon went off with a *salve tu quoque*, and a Bottle of Wine, of which the Calvinist Domine was a true Carouzer, and so we continued our *Mensalia* the whole meeting in Latine, which they both spoke so fluently and promptly that I blush'd at my self with a passionate regret, that I could not keep pace with them; and at the same time could not forbear reflecting upon our English Schools and Universities (who indeed write Latine Elegantly) but speak it, as if they were confined to Mood and Figure, Forms, and Phrases, whereas it should be their common talk in their Seats and Halls, as well as in their School Disputations, and Themes. This with all deference to these repositories of Learning. As to the Dutch Language in which I was but a smatterer, I think it lofty, majestic and emphatical, especially the German or High-Dutch, which as far as I understand it is very expressive in the Scriptures, and so underived that it may take place next the Oriental Languages, and the Septuagint: The name of the Calvinist was Newenhouse, (see Note 43), of the Lutheran Bernhardus Frazius, who was of a Gentile Personage, and a very agreeable behaviour in conversation, I seldom knew of any Law-suits, for indeed Attorneys were denyed the liberty of pleading: The English observed one anniversary custom, and that without superstition, I mean the *strenarum commercium*, as Suetonius calls them, a neighbourly commerce of presents every New-Years day.

Totus ab auspicio, ne foret annus iners. Ovid. Fastor.

Some would send me a Sugar-loaf, some a pair of Gloves, some a Bottle or two of Wine. In a word, the English Merchants and Factors (whose names are at the beginning) were very unanimous and obliging. There was one person of Quality, by name Mr. Russel, (see Note 44,) younger brother to the late Lord Russel, a gentleman of a comely Personage, and very obliging, to whose lodgings I was often welcome: But I suppose his Fortune was that of a younger Brother according to Henry the VIII's. Constitution, who abolished and repealed the Gavelkind custom, whereby the Lands of the Father were equally divided among all his Sons, so that ever since the Cadets or younger Sons of the English Nobility and Gentry, have only that of the Poet to bear up their Spirits.

Sum pauper, non culpa mea est, sed culpa parentum
Qui me fratre meo non genuere prius.

In my rude English rhiming thus.

I'm poor (my dad) but that's no fault of mine,
If any fault there be, the fault is thine,
Because thou did'st not give us Gavelkine.

The Dutch in New-York observe this custom, an instance of which I remember in one Frederick Philips (see Note 45,) the richest Miin Heer in that place, who was said to have whole Hogsheads of Indian Money or Wampam, who having one Son and Daughter, I was admiring what a heap of Wealth the Son would enjoy, to which a Dutch Man replied, that the Daughter must go halves, for so was the manner amongst them, they standing more upon Nature than Names; that as the root communicates it self to all its branches, so should the Parent to all his off-spring which are the Olive branches round about his Table. And if the case be so, the minors and infantry of the best Families might wish they had been born in Kent, rather than in such a Christendom as entails upon them their elder Brother's old Cloths, or some superannuated incumber'd reversion, but to invite both elder and younger Brothers to this sweet Climate of New-York, when they arrive there, if they are enclined to settle a Plantation, they may purchase a tract of ground at a very small rate, in my time at two-pence or three pence the Acre, for which they have a good Patent or Deed from the Governor. Indeed its all full of Wood, which as it will require some years before it be fit for use, so the burning of it does manure and meliorate the Soil; if they be for Merchandice, they pay for their freedom in New-York but fix Bevers or an equivalent in Money, i. e. three pounds twelve shillings, and seventeen shillings Fees: And Goods that are brought over commonly return cent. per cent. i. e. a hundred pounds laid out in London will commonly yield or afford 200 pounds there. Fifty per cent is looked upon as an indifferent advance, the species of payment and cerdit or trust is sometimes hazardous, and the Commodities of that Country will yield very near as much imported into England, for three and forty pounds laid out in Bever and other Furrs, when I came away, I received about four-score in London; indeed the Custom upon the skins is high, which perhaps might raise it to eight and forty pounds, or fifty; as for what I had occasion, some things were reasonable, some dear. I paid for two load of Oats in the straw 18 shillings to one Mr. Henry Dyer: to the same for a load of Pease-straw six shillings: paid to Thomas Davis for shooing my Horse three shillings, for in that place Horses are seldom, some not shod at all, their Hoofs by running in the woods so long before they are backed are like Flints: Paid to Derick, i. e. Richard Secah's Son for a load of Hay twelve shillings: Paid to Denys Fisher's Son a Carpenter, for two days work in the Stable eight shillings: for a Curry Comb and Horse-brush four shillings: to Jonathan the Barber 1*l.* 4*s.* the year: to the Shoo-maker for a pair of Boots and Shooes 1*l.* 5*s.* to the Washer-woman or Laundress 1*l.* 5*s.* 6*d.* the Year. So all Commodities and Trades are dearer or cheaper according to the plenty of importation from England and other parts: The City of New-York in my time was as large as some Market Towns with us, all built the London way; the Garrison side of a high situation and a pleasant Prospect, the Island it stands on all a level and Champain; the diversion especially in the Winter season used by the Dutch is aurigation, i. e. riding about in Wagons which is allowed by Physicians to be a very healthful exercise by Land. And upon the Ice its admirable to see Men and Women as it were flying upon their Skates from place to place, (see Note 46), with Markets upon their Heads and Backs. In a word, it's a place so every way inviting that our English Gentry, Merchants and Clergy (especially such as have the natural Stamina of a consumptive propagation in them; or an Hypocondriacal Consumption) would flock thither for self preservation. This I have all the reason to affirm, and believe from the benign effectual influence it had upon my own constitution; but oh the passage, the passage thither, *hic labor, hoc opus est:* there is the timorous objection: the Ship may founder by springing a Leak, be wreckt by a Storm or taken by a Pickeroon: which are plausible pleas to flesh and blood, but if we would examine the bills of mortality and compare the several accidents and diseases by the Land, we should find them almost a hundred for one to what happens by Sea, which deserves a particular Essay, and if we will believe the ingenious Dr. Carr in his *Epistolæ Medicinales*, there is an *Emetick Vomitory* vertue in the Sea-water it self, which by the motion of the Ship operates upon the Stomach and ejects whatever is offensive, and so extimulates and provokes or recovers the appetite, which is the chiefest defect in such Constitutions: and besides, there is a daily curiosity in contemplating the wonders of the Deep, as to see a Whale wallowing and spouting cataracts of Water, to see the Dolphin that hieroglyphick of celerity leaping above water in chase of the flying fish, which I have sometimes tasted of as they flew aboard, where they immediately expire out of their Element; and now and then to hale up that Canibal of the Sea, I mean the Shark, by the bate of a large gobbet of Beef or Pork; who makes the Deck shake again by his flapping violence, and opens his devouring mouth with double rows of teeth, in shape like a Skate or Flare as we call them in Cambridge; of which dreadful fish I have often made a meal at Sea, but indeed it was for want of other Provisions. When I came for England in a Quaker's Ship, whose Master's name was Heathcot; (see Note 47,) who, when he had his plum Broths, I and the rest were glad of what Providence sent us from day to day, our water and other Provisions, which he told us upon going aboard were fresh and newly taken in, were before we arrived in England so old and nauseous that we held our noses when we used them, and had it not been for a kind Rundlet of Medera Wine, which the Governor's Lady presented me with, it had gone worse: but such a passage may not happen once in a hundred times; for as I went from England to New-York, I faired very plentifully both with fresh and season'd meat, & good drink, Sheep killed according to our occasion, and likewise Poultry coop'd up and corn'd and cram'd, which made the common Sea men so long for a novelty, that as I went down betwixt Decks I observ'd two Terpaulins tossing something in a Blanket, and being very inquisitive they told me they were roasting a Cockerill, which was by putting a red-hot Bullet into it after it was trust, which would fetch all the Feathers off and roast well enough for their Stomachs, at which I smiling went again above-deck, and made it a publick and pardonable diversion; but as to the Sharks, as our Ship was one day becalm'd, and four of our Seamen for diversion Swimming about the Vessel, we on board espied two or three of them making towards their prey, we all shouted and made what noise we could, and scared them (tho with much ado) from seizing the Men, whilst we drew them up by ropes cast out; when they are sure of their prey they turn themselves upon their backs & strike their Prey, but in case a Man has the courage to face them in swimming they make away, so awful is the aspect of that noble animal Man: but suppose his Courage or his Strength fails him, and he becomes a prey to any of the watry host, what difference betwixt being eaten by fish or by worms at the Christian Resurrection, when the Sea must give up its Dead, and our scattered parts be recollected into the same form again; but to conclude all with an Apophthegm of the Lord Bacon's, viz. 'One was saying that his Great-Grand-father 'Grand-father and Father died at Sea. Said an-'other that heard him, and as I were you, I would 'never come to Sea; why saith he, where did 'your Great-Grand-father and Ancestors die? he 'answered where but in their Beds, saith the 'other, and I were as you I would never go to Bed. But for all this I durst venture a knap in a Cabbin at Sea, or in a Hammock in the Woods. So Reader a good Night.

Opere in tanto fas est obrepere somnum.

FINIS.

NOTES.

Note 1, *page* 21.

The good ship *Blossom* belonged to Charlestown, Mass., and was one of the "regular traders" of those days. We find that Sir Robert Carr returned to England from New York in 1667, in a vessel commanded by Captain Martin. Shortly after her arrival at New York with Gov. Andros, Robert Swet her boatswain ran away, and a "hue and cry" was sent after him from the office of the Provincial Secretary to Long Island and "The Maine." The *Blossom* cleared from New York for England on the 14th October, 1678, with the following passengers: Edward Griffith, John Delaval, Abram Depeyster, Jacques Guyon, Thomas Mollineux, Mrs. Mary Vervangher, Mrs. Frances Lowden, Mrs. Charity Clarke, Mrs. Rachel Whitthill her sister, Barent Reinderts, wife and five children, and Levynus Van Schaick; and carried back the governor's despatches. We lose sight of the good vessel now until the 6th of July, 1681, when she again arrived in New York, from which port she cleared for the Medeiras on the 1st of September following, still under the command of Capt. Richard Martin. On the 28th September, 1683, she cleared for Boston from New York; arrived at Amboy, N. J., from England, on the 15th February, 1684-5, and cleared at New York for Barbadoes on the 6th of June, 1685. From 1691 to 1701 we find the "pinke" *Blossom* a regular trader between the island of Barbadoes and New York, but under another commander.—*N. Y. State Rec.*

Note 2, *page* 21.

Sir Edmund Andros, Knight, Seigneur of Sausmarez, was born in London 6th December, 1637. His ancestors were from Northamptonshire. John Andros, the first of them connected with Guernsey, was Lieutenant to Sir Peter Meautis, the Governor, and married, in 1543, Judith de Sausmarez, the heiress, who brought the fief Sausmarez into the family. Their son, John, became a King's ward, in the custody of Sir Leonard Chamberlain, the Governor, during a long minority, and appears as a Jurat of the Royal court at the coming of the Royal Commissioners in 1582. The grandson, Thomas, also a Jurat, was Lieutenant-Governor, under Lord Carew, in 1611. He married Elizabeth, daughter of Amice de Carteret, Seigneur of Winsby Manor in Jersey, and Lieutenant-Governor and Bailiff of Guernsey, and had many children. Amice, father of Sir Edmund, was the eldest son, and married Elizabeth Stone, sister of Sir Robert Stone, Knight, Cupbearer to the Queen of Bohemia, and captain of a troop of horse in Holland; he was Master of the Ceremonies to King Charles the First when his son Edmund was born, who was brought up from a boy in the Royal family, and in its exile commenced his career of arms in Holland, under Prince Henry of Nassau. Upon the restoration of Charles the Second in 1660, the inhabitants of Guernsey thought it right to petition for pardon for having submitted to Cromwell. On the 13th August, an Order in Council was issued granting said pardon, but declaring, at the same time, that Amice Andros of Sausmarez, Bailiff of said Island, Edmund his son, and Charles, brother of Amice, had, to their great credit during the late Rebellion, continued inviolably faithful to his Majesty, and consequently, have no need of being comprised in the general pardon. To reward his loyalty, Edmund was made Gentleman in Ordinary to Elizabeth Stuart, Queen of Bohemia, the King's aunt, noted for the vicissitudes of her life, and as having given an heir to the House of Hanover; her daughter, Princess Sophia, being the mother of George the First. He subsequently distinguished himself in the war waged by Charles the Second against the Dutch, and which ended in 1667. He married in 1671, Mary, daughter of Sir Thomas Craven, a sister of Sir W. Craven, of Appletreewick in Yorkshire, and of Combe Abbey in Warwickshire, Knight, heir in reversion to the Barony of Craven of Hampsted Marshall. On 2d April, 1672, a regiment of dragoons, raised for the King's cousin, Prince Rupert, was directed to be armed "with the bayonet or great knife;" this being its first introduction into the English army. Major Andros was promoted to this regiment, and the four Barbadoes companies then under his command, were advanced to be troops of horse in it. (*Origin and Services of the Coldstream Guards, by Col. Mackinnon.*) In the same year, the proprietors of the Province of Carolina, by patent in the Latin language, dated 23d April, under their great seal and hands, and making allusion to his services and merits, conferred on him and his heirs the title and dignity of Landgrave, with four Baronies containing 48,000 acres of land at a quit-rent of a penny an acre. The distinction bestowed by the proprietors, honorable as it was, does not appear to have been otherwise beneficial, and neither he nor his heirs, it is believed, at any time derived advantage from the large quantity of land annexed to the dignity. In 1674, on the death of his father, he became Seigneur of the Fiefs and succeeded to the office of Bailiff of Guernsey, the reversion to which had been granted him. The war which had recommenced with the Dutch having terminated, his regiment was disbanded, and he was commissioned by the King to receive New York and its dependencies, pursuant to the treaty of peace, and constituted Governor of that Province. He arrived in this country, accompanied by his wife, on the 1st of November, 1674, and entered on the government on the 10th of that month. He returned to England in November, 1677, and was Knighted by Charles the Second in 1678, when he resumed his government, the affairs of which he continued to administer until

January, 1681 (N. S.), when he repaired, by order, to England, and in 1682 was sworn Gentleman of the King's Privy Chamber. In the following year, the Island of Alderney was granted to him and Lady Mary Andros, for ninety-nine years, at a rent of thirteen shillings, and in 1685 he was made Colonel of her Royal Highness Princess Anne of Denmark's regiment of horse. In 1686, James the Second appointed him Governor, Captain-General and Vice-Admiral of Massachusetts, New Hampshire, Maine, New Plymouth and certain dependent territories, and soon afterwards, in addition, of Rhode Island and of Connecticut, comprehending the whole of New England. He arrived at Nantasket in the *Kingfisher*, 50, on the 19th December, 1686, and was received, a few days after, in Boston " with great acclamation of joy." (*Cambridge Almanac*, 1687.) On the 7th April, 1688, New York and New Jersey were placed under his jurisdiction. In the month of September following, he held a Treaty with the Five Nations of Indians at Albany, and a few weeks after returned to Boston, where he had the misfortune to lose his wife in the forepart of the following year. Her Ladyship was buried by torchlight, the corpse having been carried from the Governor's residence to the South Church, in a hearse drawn by six horses, attended by a suitable guard of honor. In the administration of his government, Sir Edmund Andros failed not to become unpopular, and on the 18th April, 1689, shortly after the receipt of the news of the Revolution, he was deposed and imprisoned, and sent back to England in 1690. He continued, notwithstanding, in the favor of the Court, and in 1692 William the Third preferred him to the governorship of Virginia, to which was adjoined that of Maryland. Governor Andros brought over to Virginia the Charter of William and Mary's College, of which he laid the foundation. He encouraged manufactures and the cultivation of cotton in that Colony, regulated the Secretary's office, where he commanded all the public papers and records to be sorted and kept in order, and when the State House was burnt, had them carefully preserved and again sorted and registered. By these and other commendable acts, he succeeded in gaining the esteem of the people, and in all likelihood would have been still more useful to the Colony had his stay been longer, but his administration closed in November, 1698. (*Beverly's Virginia*, I, 37; *Oldmixon*, I, 396–398.) In 1704, under Queen Anne, he was extraordinarily distinguished by having the government of Guernsey bestowed upon him, which he held for two years; he continued Bailiff until his death, and was empowered to appoint his Lieutenant-Bailiff, who was likewise authorized to name a deputy. Sir Edmund Andros was married three times. The second wife was of the family of Crispe, which, like his own, had been attached to the Royal house in its necessities. He closed his eventful life in the parish of St. Anne, Westminster, without issue, in February, 1713 (O. S.), in his 76th year.—*N. Y. Colonial Documents*, II, 740.

Note 3, *Page* 21.

William Pinhorne had been a resident of New York previous to this time, and this was his return voyage from England. In May, 1683, he became the purchaser of the garden previously called Lovelace's Garden-house, in Broadway, N. Y., for which he paid the sum of forty pounds sterling. On the grant of a charter to the city by Governor Dongan, Mr. Pinhorne was named Alderman for the East Ward, and was elected Speaker of the Assembly which met in October, 1685. On the appointment of Sloughter to the government of New York, Mr. Pinhorne was named one of his Council, and subsequently member of the special commission which tried and condemned Leisler. In March, 1691, we find him appointed Recorder of the city of New York, and on the 5th May following, fourth justice of the Supreme Court of the Province. He held the office of Recorder until September 1, 1692, when he was removed from that, and his place in the Council, on account of non-residence. On 22d March, 1693, he became second justice of the Supreme Court, and having returned to the city of New York, was restored to his seat in the Council on 10th of June of the last mentioned year. Whilst in this situation he succeeded in securing for himself and others, an extravagant grant of land on the Mohawk river, west of Fort Hunter, fifty miles long and two miles on each side the river, at the rent of one beaver skin for the first seven years, and five beaver skins yearly for ever thereafter. But Lord Bellomont having arrived in 1698, power passed into the hands of the Leisler party, and Mr. Pinhorne was suspended, on the 7th June, from his offices of judge and councillor, on a charge of having "spoke most scandalous and reproachful words" of the King. This was followed in the course of the next year by an Act vacating his extravagant grant on the Mohawk. He now retired to his plantation on Snake Hill, on Hackensack river, N. J., and was next appointed second judge of the Supreme Court of that Province, of the Council of which he was also a member, and took his seat on the bench at Burlington in November, 1704. Here he shared all the obloquy which attached to his son-in-law, Chief Justice Mompesson. Lieutenant-Governor Ingoldesby having been removed from office, on the earnest application of the people, was succeeded by Mr. Pinhorne, who was at that time president of the Council, and who now exercised the power of commander-in-chief. The latter was superceded on the 10th June, 1710, by the arrival of Governor Hunter, and the Assembly soon after demanding his removal from all places of trust in the Province, he was dismissed in 1713. He died towards the close of 1719. Judge Pinhorne was married to Mary, daughter of Lieutenant-Governor Ingoldesby, in virtue of whose will (dated 31 August, 1711), she and her children, Mary and John, became patentees of lands in the towns of Cornwall and New Windsor, Orange county, N. Y.—*N. Y. Colonial Docs.*, III, 716.

Note 4, *Page* 21.

James Graham was a native of Scotland, and is found a resident merchant of the city of New York as early as July, 1678, and a few years later, proprietor of lands in Ulster county, Staten Island, and in New Jersey. He succeeded Mr. Rudyard as Attorney-General of the Province of New York, on 10th of December, 1685, and was sworn of the Council on the 8th of October, 1687. When the government of New England and New York were consolidated by James II, Mr. Graham removed to Boston as Attorney-General to Andros, the odium of whose government he shared, and on whose downfall he was committed to the castle. He returned to New York in 1691, where his enemies assert that he insinuated himself into the confidence of Leisler and his friends, so as to procure their interest to be chosen member of the Assembly, of which he was afterwards elected Speaker. He became, soon after, the mortal enemy of Leisler and Milborne, of whose murder he is charged, by his adversaries, with being "the principal author." Thomas Newton, Sloughter's Attorney-General, having left the Province in April, 1691, disapproving, probably, of the harsh measures of the government towards the state prisoners, George Farewell was appointed to act in his place; but this appointment not being satisfactory to the Assembly, Mr. Graham became again Attorney-General in the following May. He was about nine years Speaker of the Assembly, i. e., from 1691–1694; 1695–1698, and a part of 1699, when the friends of Leisler being in a majority, the House voted a bill of indictment, in the shape of a remonstrance, against their opponents, and had the cruelty to expect their Speaker to sign it. To enable him to avoid this unpleasant duty, Mr. Graham was called to the Council in May, 1699. His public career may be said to have now closed. He appears to have attended the Council for the last time, on the 29th July, 1700. He was superseded in October, of that year, as Recorder of the city of New York, after having filled the office from 1683, with an interruption of only two years, and was deprived of his office of Attorney-General on the 21st January, 1701, but a few days before his death, which occurred at his residence at Morrisania. His will bears date 12th January, 1700–1, and is on record in the Surrogate's office, New York. He left all his property, share and share alike, to his children, Augustine (Surveyor-General of the Province), Isabella (wife of Lewis Morris, Esq.), Mary, Sarah, Margaret and John. The other members of the family consisted, in 1698, of one overseer, two white servants and thirty-three slaves.—*New York Colonial Documents*, IV, 847. On the 18th July, 1684, a license of Marriage was issued out of the Provincial Secretary's office, New York, for James Graham and Elizabeth Windebauke.—*N. Y. Colonial MSS.*, XXXIII, pt. ii, p. 32. But whether it refers to the Attorney-General whose biography is now sketched, we have no means of ascertaining.

Note 5, *Page* 21.

John West had been a resident of New York during Governor Andros' first administration, and is found acting as a lawyer there as early as 1675. In the following year, he received the appointment of deputy clerk of the Mayor's court, and clerk of the Sessions for the North and West Ridings of Yorkshire, and was employed in a legal capacity to assist the commission appointed to examine into the condition of Governor Lovelace's estate. He seems next to have gone back to England, but on returning to New York, is again found enjoying the confidence and patronage of the government, being employed as member of the Court of Admiralty at Nantucket; justice of the peace at Pemaquid, &c. In 1680 he received the appointment of clerk of the Council, Secretary of the Province, clerk to the Court of Assizes, and clerk of the city of New York, but in 1683, he was superseded by James Spragg as Provincial secretary and clerk of the Court of Assizes. The latter tribunal, however, was soon after abolished, but Mr. West retained his city appointment and received also that of clerk of the Sessions. In October, 1684, he married Anne Rudyard, daughter of the Lieutenant-Governor of East Jersey, and in 1685 was commissioned to claim Westfield, Northampton, Deerfield and other towns on the west side of Connecticut river, for the Duke of York. When Sir Edmund Andros, his patron, returned to power in 1686–7, Mr. West accompanied him to Boston; there he farmed from Edward Randolph the office of secretary, in which capacity he extorted what fees he pleased, to the great oppression of the people, and thus aided in rendering the government odious. On the overthrow of that government, West was seized and committed to the castle at Boston. Many of the charges against him are given in the tract entitled "The Revolution of New England Justified." After a protracted confinement, it appears that he was shipped off to England in 1690. Of his subsequent career I have no knowledge; but I apprehend that he did not long survive his downfall. His widow afterwards became the wife of Robert Wharton.—The above details are collected from the *N. Y. Records* in the office of the Secretary of State, Albany; *Byfield's Account of the late Revolution; N. Y. Colonial Documents*, III; and *Hutchinson's History of Massachusetts.*

Note 6, *page* 21.

Peter Heylin, D. D., was born in Burford, Oxfordshire, on 29th Nov., 1599, and in 1613 entered Hart Hall, Oxford; took the degree of B. A. in 1617, and was chosen Fellow in 1619. Having already given a course of lectures on Cosmography, he composed his Microcosmus, which was published in 1621, 4to)*Watts*); 1622 (*Wood*) small 4to. He received holy orders in 1623, and in 1624–5, a second edition of his Microcosmus appeared, with augmentations and corrections. He visited France in 1625, and on his return wrote an account of his journey, which was published some 30 years subsequent to his visit. In 1627, a third edition of the Microcosmus was published. In 1629 he was nominated one of the king's chaplains, and in 1631 made rector of Henningford, Huntingdonshire, and a prebend of Westminster. The year following, he obtained the rich living of Houghton in the Spring, which he changed for Ailresford, Hampshire; in 1633 proceeded to D. D., and in 1638, exchanged for South Warnborough, Hants. On the breaking out of the civil war, Dr. Heylin abandoned his rectories and followed the king to Oxford, where he became one of the editors of the Weekly Newspaper, called the *Mercurius Aulicus*, then published on the royal side. In 1643, his property was sequestered by order of the Parliament, and he thus lost his incomparable library. Now he was obliged to shift from place to place to escape his enemies, and finally settled down in Minster Level, where he was forced "to the earning of money by writing books." Here, he prepared the first folio edition of his Cosmography, which was published in 1652. He next removed to Abendon, in order to have easier access to libraries, for he found it (he says) as difficult to make books without books, as the Israelites, to make bricks without straw. At length, at the restoration, this worthy old loyalist was restored to his spiritualities. Though the list of Dr. Heylin's works is considerable, he is best known in this country by his "Cosmographie." It was the last book that its author wrote with his own hand (in 1651), for after it was finished, his eyes failed him so that he could neither see to write nor read, and was forced to employ an amanuensis. At length, after a life chequered by adversity and prosperity, he paid his last debt to nature on Ascension day, the 8th of May, 1662, and was buried within the choir of St. Peter's Church, Westminster. A copy of the inscription on his monument is in *Hist. and Antiq. Univ. Oxon.*, and a list of his works is in *Wood's Athen. Oxon.* II, 183, *et seq.*

Note 7, *page* 21.

Richard Nicolls was the fourth son of Francis Nicolls, who is described in a pedigree of the family entered in the Heralds' College in 1628, as "of the Middle Temple, one of the Squiers of the Bath to Sir Edward Bruse, and lyeth buried at Ampthill, co. Bedford." His mother was Margaret, daughter of Sir George Bruce of Carnock, Knt., the lineal ancestor of the present Earl of Elgin, and younger brother of Sir Edward Bruce, the favorite servant of James I, and his Master of the Rolls. Richard Nicolls was born in the year 1624, probably at Ampthill, at which place his father was buried in the same year. Ampthill great park was a royal chase, the custody of which was granted, in 1613, by King James I, to Thomas, Lord Bruce, whose son, Robert Bruce, was created in 1664 Viscount Bruce of Ampthill, and Earl of Aylesbury. In the seventeenth century the Nicollses were for many years lessees of Ampthill Park under the Bruce family, and resided at the Great Lodge, or Capital Mansion, as it is called in the survey of 1649. Here Richard Nicolls passed his boyhood under the charge of his mother, who survived her husband, and remained a widow until her death in 1652. He had two brothers, who survived their father, the one, Edward, ten years, and the other, Francis, five years older than himself. His only sister, Bruce, was thirteen years of age at the time of his birth, and was married shortly after to John Frecheville (son and heir apparent of Sir John Frecheville of Staveley, co. Derby, Knt.), who, in 1664, was created Baron Frecheville of Staveley. She died in 1629, without issue, at the age of eighteen.

The breaking out of the civil war in 1642 found Richard Nicolls at the university, where, if we can accept the testimony of the epitaph on his monument in Ampthill church, he acquired some distinction in his studies. He was not permitted, however, to pursue this career; but in 1643, at the youthful age of eighteen, he was called away to take part in the civil war, which was then actively waging. As might be supposed from his connections, the sympathies and affections of Richard Nicolls were engaged on the royal side. His mother was one of the family—itself connected with the royal line—which had been caressed and enriched by King James. His uncle, Dr. William Nicolls, a dignitary of the English Church, was indebted to the favor of King Charles for his preferments, having been presented in 1623 to the living of Cheadle in Chester, by Charles, Prince of Wales and Earl of Chester, to whom the presentation had fallen by lapse, and was advanced in 1644 to the Deanery of Chester.

Richard Nicolls joined the royal forces, in which he received the command of a troop of horse. Each of his brothers commanded a company of infantry on the same side, and distinguished himself by his devotion to the royal cause; but the favor which their services gained them was more honorable than advantageous. They shared the exile of the royal family, and following their banished king in his wanderings, Edward, the elder brother, died at Paris, and Francis at the Hague. During the period following the death of King Charles, when the royal family remained in Paris, Richard Nicolls was attached to the service of James, Duke of York, whose attendants, as we learn from Clarendon, shared in a more than ordinary degree in the distresses, and also in the disorder and faction which prevailed in the banished court. In the spring of 1652, the Duke of York obtained the permission of his brother and his council to join the army under the Marshal Turenne, then engaged in the war of the Fronde. Richard Nicolls accompanied him, and had thus an opportunity, to adopt the words of the Cardinal Mazarin in proposing to the queen to send her son to the wars, of "learning his *mestier*, under a general reputed equal to any captain in Christendom." The duke afterwards served upon the other side under Don John of Austria and the Prince de Conde, and we may conjecture that he was followed throughout these campaigns by Nicolls, who, on the return of the royal family to their country in 1660, was appointed one of the gentlemen of the bedchamber to the duke.

In 1664, war with Holland being then imminent, the king granted to his brother the Duke of York, the country in North America then occupied by the Dutch Settlement of New Netherland. The grant to the Duke of York is dated the 12th of March, 1664, and it comprises Long Island, and "all the land from the west side of Connecticut river to the east side of Delaware bay, and the islands known by the names of Martin's Vineyard or Nantucks, otherwise Nantucket." Part of this tract was conveyed away by the duke to Lord Berkeley of Stratton and George Carteret of Saltrum, co. Devon, by lease and release dated the 22d and 23d of June, 1664, and received the name of New Jersey from its connection with the Carteret family.

Letters patent were issued on the 25th of April, 1664, appointing Colonel Richard Nichols, Sir Robert Carr, Knt., George Cartwright and Samuel Maverick, Esquires, Commissioners, with power for them, or any three or two of them, or the survivors of them, of whom Colonel Richard Nichols, during his life, should be always one, and should have a casting vote, to visit all the colonies and plantations within the tract known as New England, and "to heare and determine all complaints and appeales in all causes and matters, as well military as criminal and civil, and proceed in all things for the providing for and settleing the peace and security of the said country according to their good and sound discretion, and to such instructions as they or the successors of them have, or shall from time to time receive for us in that behalfe, and from time to time to certify us or our privy council of their actings and proceedings touching the premisses."

The instructions furnished to Colonel Nicolls respecting his proceedings with the Dutch, required him to reduce them to the same obedience with the king's subjects in those parts, without using any other violence than was necessary to those ends; and if necessary, "to use such force as could not be avoided for their reduction, they having no kind of right to hold what they are in possession of in our unquestionable territories, than that they are possessed of by an invasion of Us."

The expedition under Nicolls set sail from Portsmouth in June, 1664. It consisted of four frigates, and about 300 soldiers. Colonel Nicolls, on board the Guyny, arrived at Boston on the 27th July, and required assistance towards reducing the Dutch. The council of the town agreed to furnish 200 men, but the object was effected by Nicolls before this force joined him. On the 20th August, his force being now collected at Long Island, Nicolls summoned the Dutch governor to surrender. Stuyvesant, the governor, would willingly have defended the town, but there was no disposition in the burghers to support him; and a capitulation was signed on 27th by Commissioners on each side, and confirmed by Nicolls. In the course of the next month, Sir Robert Carr and Col. Cartwright reduced all the remaining Dutch settlements in New Netherland.

Upon the reduction of New Amsterdam, Nicolls assumed the government of the province, now called New York, under the style of "Deputy-Governor under his royal highness the Duke of York, of all his territories in America." The American authorities are generally agreed that his rule, though somewhat arbitrary, was honest and salutary. English forms and methods of government were gradually introduced; and in June, 1665, the scout, burgomasters and schepens of the Dutch municipality were superseded by a mayor, aldermen, and sheriff. His administration lasted three years, and his mode of proceeding is thus summed up by William Smith, the historian of New York: "He erected no courts of justice, but took upon himself the sole decision of all controversies whatever. Complaints came before him by petition; upon which he gave a day to the parties, and after a summary hearing, pronounced judgment. His determinations were called edicts, and executed by the sheriffs he had appointed. It is much to his honor, that, notwithstanding all this plenitude of power, he governed the province with integrity and moderation. A representation from the inhabitants of Long Island to the General Court of Connecticut, made about the time of the Revolution, commends him, as a man of an easy and benevolent disposition; and this is the more to be relied upon, because the design of the writers was, by a detail of their grievances, to induce the colony of Connecticut to take them under its immediate protection." In a letter to the Duke of York, dated November, 1665, Colonel Nicolls thus expresses himself: "My endeavors have not been wanting to put the whole government into one frame and policy, and now the most factious republicans can not but acknowledge themselves fully satisfied with the way and method they are in."

Nicolls returned to England in 1667, and resumed his position in the Duke of York's household. In 1672 war was again proclaimed against the Dutch. The distinction between the land and sea services was not then established, and several landsmen volunteered to serve in the fleet, which was commanded by the Duke of York, the Earl of Sandwich, and the Count D'Estrees. Among these volunteers were several of the Lord High Admiral's household, and among the number Colonel Richard Nicolls. In the engagement which took place at Solebay, on the 28th of May, 1672, in which Lord Sandwich lost his life by the blowing up of the ship which he commanded, Colonel Nicolls, with Sir John Fox, the Captain of the Royal Prince, in which he sailed, and others of the volunteers, was also killed. His age at the time of his death was forty-seven.

Colonel Nicolls left no legitimate issue, and, I believe, was never married. His will, dated the 1st of May, 1672, on board the Royal Prince at the Nore, was proved by his executors in the Prerogative Court of Canterbury in the following June. He desires to be buried at Ampthill, and alms to be given to the parishes through which his funeral would pass, and a marble monument to be erected to his memory, with an inscription mentioning his father and mother, his brother William, and his brothers Edward and Francis, the one dead at the Hague, the other at Paris during the late usurpation; and his executors might add what they pleased about his own services in America and elsewhere. He prays his executors to be "earnest solicitors with his Highness for the money due to him."

His executors fulfilled his injunctions by erecting a white marble monument to his memory in the north-east corner of the chancel of Ampthill church, in the upper part of which the cannon ball which caused his death is enclosed, with the words "*Instrumentum mortis et immortalitatis.*" The inscription on the monument is as follows:

M. S.
Optimis parentibus nunc tumulo conjunctus
Pietate semper conjunctissimus
Hic jacet
Richardus Nicolls Francisci Istius ex Margar. Bruce
filius,
Illimo Jacobo Duci Ebor. a Cubiculis intimis;
Anno 1643, relictis musarum castris,
Turmam equestrem contra rebelles duxit.
Juvenis strenuus atque impiger.
Anno 1664, ætate jam et scientia militari maturus,
In AMERICAM
Septentrionalem cum imperio missus
Longam I's'lam cœterasque insulas
Belgis expulsis vero Domino restituit,
Provinciam arcesque munitissimas
Heri sui titulis insignivit,
Et triennio pro preside rexit
Academia Literis
Bello Virtute
Aula Candore animi
Magistratu Prudentia
Celebris,
ubique bonis charus, sibi et negotiis par.
28 Maii 1672
nave prætoria contra eosd. Belgas
fortiter dimicans,
ictu globi majoris transfossus occubuit.
Fratres habuit,
præter Gulielmum præcoci fato defunctum,
Edvardum et Franciscum
utrumque copiarum pedestrium centurionem,
Qui fœdæ et servilis tyrannidis
quæ tunc Angliam oppresserat impatientes,
exilio prælato (si modo regem extorrem sequi exil: sit)
alter Parisiis, alter Haga comitis,
ad cœlestem patriam migrârunt.

Above are the Nicolls arms: Azure, a fess between three lions' heads or; Crest, a tiger sejant.—2 *Notes and Queries*, III, 214; *Nichols's Topographer and Genealogist*, III, 539–544.

Note 8, *page* 22.

Mere discovery of a country, not followed by actual possession, confers no title. This principle of public law was laid down and acted upon by Elizabeth, Queen of England, as far back as 1580, when resisting the exclusive pretensions of Spain to the New World. "As she did not acknowledge the Spaniards to have any title by donation of the Bishop of Rome, so she knew no right they had to any places other than those they were in actual possession of; for their having touched only here and there upon a coast, and given names to a few rivers, or capes, were such insignificant things as could in no ways entitle them to a propriety, farther than in the parts where they actually settled, and continued to inhabit."* The right derived from the Cabots, which had not even the plea of "having touched here and there on a coast" to support it, thus falling to the ground—for what was good as against Spain for England, must be admitted good also against the latter for the Dutch—the only remaining title in favor of England to this continent rests on the colonization of Virginia. This did not extend farther north than the Chesapeake or James river. Actual settlement and continual habitation, which Queen Elizabeth laid down as necessary to make out a title, were, therefore, wanting to establish the English right to the country first discovered and now actually possessed by the Dutch. To call these "intruders," was, in the words of Louis XIV, "a species of mockery;" they had as good a right to reclaim the American wilderness as any other European power, and so long as they could show all the prerequisites insisted on by England in 1580 to establish a title, theirs must be considered unobjectionable. This view of the case is only strengthened by an examination of the New England patent, granted by James I to the Plymouth Company. This charter conveyed all the country from forty to forty-eight degrees of north latitude, with this express reservation, however: "Provided, always, that the said islands, or any of the said premises hereinbefore mentioned, . . . be not actually possessed or inhabited by any other Christian Prince or Estate." The Dutch had actual possession of New Netherland many years before the issue of this patent, and the reservation in favor of the rights of others which that document contains, was a full and perfect acknowledgment of the soundness of their title.†—*O'Callaghan's History of New Netherland*, II, 343-4.

---

* Camden, Rerum Anglicarum et Hibernicarum Annales, regnante Elizabetha, 8vo. Leyden, 1639, p. 328. "Proscriptio sine possessione haud valeat," was the principle laid down in this case.

† See Patent in Hazard, I, 111. Consult further, "A State and Representation of the Bounds of the Province of New York against the claim of the Province of the Massachusetts Bay," &c., in the Journals of the New York Prov. Assembly; also, Lettres du Comte d'Estrades, Lond. 8vo. 1748, III, 340, for the letter of the King of France, in which he states that after examination of both sides of the question, the right of the Dutch to the country is, in his estimation, the best established—"le mieux fondé."

Note 9, page 22.

SEBASTIAN CABOT, an eminent navigator, was the son of John Cabot, a Venetian. The place of his birth has been a subject for some difference of opinion; some claiming the honor for Venice; others, for Bristol, England. In 1497, when about twenty years of age, he accompanied his father in the voyage in which the continent of the New World was discovered. In the year 1498, he made another voyage to this continent, which he reached somewhere between the 55th and 67th degrees of latitude, when he sailed south and returned home. About the year 1517 he sailed on another voyage of discovery, and went to the Brazils, and thence to Hispaniola and Porto Rico. Failing in his object of finding a way to the East Indies, he returned to England. Having been invited to Spain, where he was received in the most respectful manner by King Ferdinand and Queen Isabella, he made a voyage of discovery in April, 1525; visited the coast of Brazil, and entered a great river, to which he gave the name of Rio de la Plata. He sailed up this river one hundred and twenty leagues. After being absent on this expedition a number of years, he returned to Spain in the spring of 1531. He made other voyages, of which no particular memorials remain. His residence was at the city of Seville. His employment as Chief Pilot was the drawing of charts, on which he delineated all the new discoveries made by himself and others; and, by his office, he was entrusted with the reviewing of all projects for discovery. His character is said to have been gentle, friendly, and social, though in his voyages some instances of injustice towards the natives and of severity towards his mariners, are recorded. In his advanced age he returned to England; received a pension from Edward VI, and was appointed governor of a company of merchants, associated for the purpose of making discoveries. He had a strong persuasion that a passage might be found to China by the northeast. By his means a trade was commenced with Russia, which gave rise to the Russian company. The last account of him is, that in 1556, when the company were sending out a vessel for discovery, he made a visit on board. "The good old gentleman, master Cabota," says the journal of the voyage in Hakluyt, "gave to the poor most liberal alms, wishing them to pray for the good fortune and prosperous success of our pinnace. And then at the sign of St. Christopher, he and his friends banqueted, and for very joy, that he had to see the towardness of our intended discovery, he entered into the dance himself among the rest of the young and lusty company; which being ended, he and his friends departed, most gently commending us to the governance of Almighty God." He died shortly afterwards, at the age of 80 years, but the place where he was buried is not known. He was one of the most extraordinary men of the age in which he lived. There is preserved in Hakluyt a complete set of instructions, drawn and signed by Cabot, for the direction of the voyage to Cathay in

China, which affords the clearest proof of his sagacity. It is supposed that he was the first who noticed the variations of the magnetic needle. He published also a large map, which was engraved by Clement Adams, and hung up in the gallery at Whitehall; and on this map was inscribed a Latin account of the discovery of Newfoundland.—*Belknap's Amer. Biog.*, I, 149–158; *Mass. Mag.*, II, 467–471; *Hakluyt*, I, 226, 268, 274; *Campbell's Admirals*, I, 419; *Rees' Cyclopedia; Petri Martyr. De Novo Orbe, Paris*, 1587, pp. 232, 589; *Bancroft's Hist. U. States*, I, 7–14; 2 *Notes and Queries*, V, 1, 154, 193, 263, 285.

Note 10, *page* 22.

Sir John Vaughan, Kt., was born in Cardiganshire in 1608, and educated at Worcester school and at Christchurch, Oxford, whence he removed to the Inner Temple, where he contracted an intimacy with Selden, who made him one of his executors. During the Rebellion, he led a retired life, but at the Restoration was elected to Parliament for Cardiganshire. In 1668, he became Chief Justice of the Common Pleas, and died in 1674. His reports and arguments were published in 1677, by his son, Edward Vaughan, Esq., in 1 vol. folio.

Note 11, *page* 22.

The precise Latitude of the City Hall, New York, is 40 deg., 42 min., 43 sec.; Longitude west from Greenwich Observatory, 74 deg., 3 sec. See *Map B, No.* 2, *Hudson River* (lower sheet); accompanying *Report of the U. S. Coast Survey during the year* 1855. Washington: Nicholson. 1856.

Note 12, *page* 22.

Richard Norwood is principally famous for having been one of the first who measured a degree of the Meridian. He wrote Trignometry, or Doctrine of Triangles; Fortification; the Seaman's Practice; Epitome and Logarithmic Tables; also, Letters and Papers in the Philosophical Transactions on the Tides and on the Whale Fishery.

Andrew Norwood his son had been a resident of the West Indies, and communicated to the Royal Society, in 1668, "Observations in Jamaica." He seems to have immigrated to New York before the assumption of the government by Sir Edmund Andros; for, in March, 1672, an order was issued to lay out two towns or townships on Staten Island, and in September following he received a grant of one hundred and fifty acres of land on the shore of Staten Island, near the present Quarantine ground. On the 29th of September, 1676, this grant was increased by Governor Andros to three hundred and ninety-seven acres. In September, 1677, he received an additional grant of twenty-five acres, making his farm four hundred and twenty acres in all.—*N. Y. Patents.* In 1677 he was appointed surveyor of that locality, as appears by the following

Commission for Mr. Andrew Norwood to be Surveyor for Staten Island.

By the Governor.

These are to authorize and Appoint you Mr. Andrew Norwood to be Surveyor of Staten Island, where you are to Survey and lay out such Lotts or Parcels of land, as you shall be employed about, of which to make due returnes according to Law, And in all matters relating thereunto to behave yourselfe according to the duty and place of Surveyor. Given under my hand in New Yorke, this 12th day of November, 1677.

E. ANDROS. S.

N. Y. Warrants, Orders, Passes, &c., 1674–1678, XXXII, 291.

It appears that Mr. Norwood returned to, and died in, the West Indies; for, I find that his will, dated 24th of April, 1684, was admitted to probate in the island of St. Christopher. In virtue of this will, the above mentioned property on Staten Island, came into the possession of his son, Henry Norwood of Jamaica, who sold it in 1697, to Antony Bigg of Port Royal, for the sum of £300 Jamaica currency. Biggs sold the property to John Stout of the same place, in 1698, for an advance of about £10.—*N. Y. Deed Book*, IX, 584. This transaction will, when compared with present prices, afford an opportunity of forming an idea of the advance in value of real estate on Staten Island.

Note 13, *page* 22.

Philip Wells. The earliest notice that I can find of this gentleman is in the year 1675, when he was authorized to receive the county rates in the absence of Sheriff Salisbury, who had gone to England. Hence it is inferred, that he came to New York in 1674 with Governor Andros, whose "Steward" he is said to have been. In 1676, he was appointed receiver of the debts due to the late Dutch West India Company, and is next called "Commissary to the Garrison of Fort James at New York," in which capacity he is empowered to draw from the collector of that city such duties as that officer might receive, in order to support the garrison and pay other expenses of government. On the 26th Nov., 1680, Mr. Wells was appointed Surveyor. He became, in 1684, Surveyor-General of the Province and held that office until 1687. He was one of the commissioners who ran the boundary line between Connecticut and New York in 1684, and being a landed proprietor on Staten Island, is found in the commission of the peace for the county of Richmond in 1685. In 1686, he was appointed surveyor on the part of New York, to determine, with similar functionaries on the behalf of East and West Jersey, the most northerly branch of the Delaware river, and to run a line between these three provinces. No line, however, was actually run. The instructions to "Philip Wells, Esq., Surveyor-General of His Majesty's Province of New York," are in *N. Y. Council Minutes*, V. It was on the occasion of this commission, we presume, that he observed the declination of the magnetic needle, as mentioned by Kalm in his notice of

New York. On quitting the office of Surveyor-General, Mr. Wells retired to Staten Island, where we find him residing in 1694.—*N. Y. State Records.*

Note 14, *page* 23.

SIR HENRY WOTTON was born at Bocton Hall, Kent, and educated at Winchester and Oxford. He subsequently became secretary to the Earl of Essex, but on the fall of that nobleman, retired to the continent. He returned to England on the accession of James I, by whom he was knighted, and sent Ambassador to Venice, and several other courts. He was afterwards appointed Provost of Eton, took holy orders, and died in 1639. These words are engraved on his tomb: Hic jacet hujus sententiæ primus auctor: Disputandi pruritus, ecclesiæ scabies. Nomen alias quære. He wrote, The State of Christendom; Elements of Architecture; Parallels between Essex and Buckingham; Characters of some of the Kings of England; Essays on Education; Poems, printed in the Reliquiæ Wottoniæ; Two Apologies relating to his Album Aphorism: An Ambassador is an honest man sent to lie abroad for the good of his country. Some of his religious poems are exquisitely beautiful; that written On a Bed of Sickness, has never been surpassed.—*Rose.* Sir Dudley Carleton gave him the soubriquet of Fabritio.—2 *Notes and Queries*, VII, 375.

Note 15, *page* 24.

GEORGE HAKEWELL, D. D., was born in Exeter, England, in 1578, and received the rudiments of his education in that city. He entered Oxford as a commoner in 1595, and in two years after was elected a Fellow of Exeter college. Having received holy orders he traveled on the continent of Europe, and in 1610, received his divinity degree. In 1611, he was appointed chaplain to Prince Charles, and archdeacon of Surrey in 1616. He subsequently opposed the marriage of the Infanta of Spain with the Prince, in consequence of which he was dismissed from his chaplaincy in 1621. He afterwards was appointed rector of Heanton, Devonshire, and in 1641 was elected rector of Exeter college. On the civil war breaking out, he gave in his submission to parliament, and spent the remainder of his days in retirement at Heanton, where he died in the beginning of April, 1649. His remains were deposited in the chancel of his church, and over his grave a stone was laid with this Inscription: Reliquiæ Georgii Hakewell, S. Th. D. Archidiaconi Surriæ, collegii Exoniensis et hujus Ecclesiæ Rectoris, in spem resurrectionis hic repositæ sunt, An. 1649. ætatis suæ 72. A list of his works is in *Wood's Athenæ Oxon.*, II, 66. The most important of his writings is: An Apology or Declaration of the Power and Providence of God in the Government of the World, 1627, folio. The learning exhibited in this work is very extensive.—*Rose, Biog. Dict.*, VIII, 174.

Note 16, *page* 27.

WILLIAM ASHFORDBY is supposed to have come to this country in 1664. In 1676 he obtained a patent for one hundred and eight acres of land in Marbletown (Ulster co.), in the neighborhood of "the Indian graves." On the 21st of December, 1684, he was appointed High Sheriff of Ulster county, and obtained a further grant of eighty-seven acres and a half of land in the rear of the tract first above mentioned. Yet with all this, whether through want of thrift or of industry, Mr. Ashfordby did not prosper. He became considerably indebted; had to mortgage his property, and in 1687, the High Sheriff of Ulster county "went for England," leaving behind him his debts and a wife and family. In August, 1695, a petition was presented to the Governor and Council of New York, from his wife Martha, in behalf of herself and five children, John Bettis and Susannah his wife, Mary, Helen, Ann, and Catherine Ashfordby, setting forth the fact of his absconding, and praying a grant of the last mentioned tract, for herself and children. She received a patent accordingly. Mr. Ashfordby having left no male issue, the name has become extinct in Ulster co.—*N. Y. Patents*, IV, 51, VI, 539; *N. Y. Col. MSS.*, XXX, 61, XXXI, iii, 83, XL, 56; *Council Minutes*, VII, 153.

Note 17, *page* 27.

SOPUS, or Esopus, lies on the west side of the Hudson river, 90 miles north of the city of New York. The name belonged originally to the river which discharges into the Hudson at this point, and is a modification of the Algonquin word *Sipous*, the literal signification of which, is "River." The first Dutch adventurers traded with the Indians here as early as 1614, and though that trade was carried on continuously afterwards, there is no evidence of any improvement having been made thereabouts before 1652–3. The neglect of the government to extinguish the Indian title to the land before parcelling it out to actual settlers, led to two wars with the Aborigines, and greatly retarded the advancement of the place, which was not erected into a municipality until 1661, when the district went by the Dutch name of *Wiltwyck*, or Indianville. Governor Lovelace, however, was the chief promoter of the settlement of the Esopus. For, orders having been given to disband the soldiers who had accompanied Colonel Nicolls to this country, gratuitous grants of land were made to them in 1668, and two new towns planted. On the 18th September, 1669, by the governor's orders, one was called "Marbleton" and the other "Hurley;" the latter, after the seat of the Lovelace family in Berkshire, England. On the 25th of the same month, *Wiltwyck*, or "the towne formerly called Sopez, was named KINGSTON;" some suppose out of respect to the king; others, however, are of opinion that the name was borrowed from that of Kingston L'Isle, Berkshire, the seat of the first Lady Lovelace's family. When the Dutch recovered the country in 1673, the name of Kingston was changed to *Swaenenburgh*, and so continued until the English returned under Governor Andros, in 1674. The district was organized into a distinct county in 1683, by an act of the Provincial Legislature, and was called Ulster, to commemorate the Irish title of the Duke of York, who was Earl of Ulster in the peerage of Ireland.—*O'Callaghan's Hist. New Netherland; N. Y. Colonial MSS.*, XXII, 99; *Laws of New York;* see Note 16 *supra.*

Note 18, *page* 27.

William Harvey, M. D., famous for his discovery of the Circulation of the Blood, was born in Folkestone, Kent, 2d April, 1578. Having finished his education at Cambridge, he passed through several celebrated medical schools on the continent, took his degree in 1602, and commenced practice in London, where he made his great discovery about the year 1619. He afterwards became physician to James I and Charles I. On the breaking out of the civil war he retired to Richmond, and in 1651 appeared his second immortal work: Exercitationes de Generatione Animalium. 4to. This great man died 3d July, 1658, in the 80th year of his age. A monument has been erected to his memory at Hempstead in Essex. A splendid quarto edition of all his works was published by the College of Physicians in 1766, to which a life of the author is prefixed.—*Rose.*

Note 19, *page* 27.

George Carew, was the son of the dean of Exeter and Windsor, of the same name. Adopting the profession of arms, he was in the expedition to Cadiz, in 1588–9, and afterwards served with great reputation in Ireland, where he was made President of Munster, when, uniting his forces with those of the Earl of Thomond, he reduced several castles and strong places, and obtained many triumphs. He was likewise a privy councillor in that kingdom. Upon the accession of James I, he was constituted lieutenant-general of the ordnance, and governor of the Isle of Guernsey, and having married Joyce, only daughter and heiress of William Clopton, Esq., of Clopton in the county of Warwick, was elevated to the peerage, on the 4th June, 1605, as Baron Carew. He was made master-general of the ordnance in 1609, and sworn of the privy council, and in 1625 created Earl of Totness. "Besides," says Dugdale, "these his noble employments, 'tis not a little observable, that, being a great lover of antiquities, he wrote an historical account of all those memorable passages, which hapned in Ireland, during the term of those three years, he continued there, intituled *Hibernia Pacata*, printed at London, in 1633, and that he made an ample collection of many chronological and choice observations, as also of divers exact maps, relating to sundry parts of that realm, some whereof are now in the public library at Oxford, but most of them in the hands of Sir Robert Shirley, Bart., of Stanton Harold, in the county of Leicester, bought of his executors." His lordship died 27th March, 1629, at the Savoy in the Strand, "in the suburbs of London," leaving an only daughter and heiress.—*Burke; Beatson.*

Note 20, *page* 28.

Charles Blount, eighth Baron Mountjoy of Thurveston, in the county of Derby, succeeded to the title on the death of his brother in 1594. This nobleman, when a commoner, being a person of high military reputation, had a command in the fleet which defeated the famous Spanish Armada, and a few years afterwards succeeded the Earl of Sussex in the governorship of Portsmouth. In 1597, his lordship was constituted Lieutenant of Ireland; and in two years afterwards repulsed the Spaniards, with great gallantry, at Kinsale. Upon the accession of James I, he was reinvested with the same important office, and created, by letters patent, dated 21st July, 1603, Earl of Devonshire, being made at the same time a Knight of the most noble order of the Garter. The high public character of the earl was, however, considerably tarnished by one act of his private life, the seduction of Penelope, sister of the Earl of Essex, and wife of Robert, Lord Rich. By this lady he had several children; and upon his return from Ireland, finding her divorced from her husband, he married her, at Wanstead in Essex, on the 26th of December, 1605, the ceremony being performed by his chaplain, Wiliam Laud, afterward Archbishop of Canterbury. Camden says, that this nobleman was so eminent for valor and learning, that in those respects, "he had no superior, and but few equals," and his secretary Moryson, writes, "that he was beautiful in person as well as valiant; and learned as well as wise." His lordship died on the 3d April, 1606, and leaving no legitimate issue, all his honors became extinct.—*Burke, Ext. and Dorm. Peerage.*

Note 21, *Page* 29.

Aberginians. The several scattered tribes from the Pockanockets of Plymouth colony to the Piscataqua river, were called Northern Indians, and by some Aberginians.—*Hutchinson's Mass.*, I, 407. The name enters into Mr. Gallatin's vocabulary as an Indian word (*Synopsis of Indian Tribes*, 312), but it seems to be rather a corruption of Aborigines.

Note 22, *page* 30.

William Camden, a learned antiquary, was born in the Old Bailey, London, on the 2d May, 1551. He received the first rudiments of knowledge at Christchurch Hospital, and was afterwards sent to Dr. Colet's free school, near St.

Paul's. In 1566, he was sent to the university at Oxford, where he remained until 1571, when he returned to London. In 1575 he obtained the place of second master of Westminster school. He now devoted himself to his favorite studies, and in 1582 brought out his Britannia: sive Regnorum Angliæ, Scotiæ, Hiberniæ, and Insularum adjacentium Descriptio; 8vo.; Maps. In 1593, he was made head master of Westminster school, and published a Greek Grammar in 1597. The first part of the Annals of Queen Elizabeth appeared in 1615, under this title—Rerum Anglicarum and Hibernicarum Annales regnante Elizabetha; the second half followed in 1627, after the author's death; both were published in London in folio. After passing through several editions, this work was translated into English and printed also in folio. After a life of great literary industry and labor, he paid his last debt to nature at Chiselhurst, Kent, on the 9th November, 1623. His remains were interred in Westminster Abbey, where a monument, with a suitable inscription, was erected to his memory. A full list of Camden's works will be found in *Wood's Athen. Oxon.* I, 412.

Note 23, *page* 30.

Stephen Skinner, M. D., was born in or near London in 1623, and entered Christ church, Oxon, in 1638, but before he could obtain a degree, the rebellion broke out, so that he was obliged to resort to the continent to continue his studies. In 1646, he returned to Oxford and took both the degrees in arts, and subsequently received the degree of Doctor of Medicine from the university of Heidelberg, and was admitted *ad eundem* by the university at Oxford, in 1664, in which year he settled at Lincoln, where he practised his profession. He died in that city on the 5th September, 1667, and was buried in the cathedral. His works were published in one folio volume at London, in 1671, with this title: Etymologicon linguæ Anglicanæ, under the care and superintendence of Mr. Thomas Henshaw, a learned critic.—*Wood's Athen. Oxon.* II, 287.

Note 24, *page* 33.

For an interesting account of Indian currency, the reader is referred to Denton's Brief Description of New York: formerly called New Netherland. New York: Gowans, 1845. 8vo p. 42.

Note 25, *page* 34.

The following clippings from newspapers, show the prices of Negro slaves in this country in 1859:

Sale of Negroes—High Prices.—Twenty-eight negroes were sold on Tuesday last, at McDonough, in Henry county, Va. The aggregate amount of the sales was $22,309, being an average of $796. We select the following from the list, as an evidence of the high prices paid: One boy, field hand, 18 years old, $1,640; three boys, 14 years old—one $1,440, one $1,282, another $1,207; two boys, 10 years old—one $902, the other $806; one 7 years old, $726, one woman, 23 years old, with three boys—one 5 years, one 3 years, and one 8 months, $1,995; one woman, 23 years old, with two children—a boy 3 years, a girl 18 months old, $2,305; seven girls sold at the following prices—one 19 years old, $1,200; one 15 years, $1,023; one 16 years, $1,100; one 12 years, $400; one 7 years, $705; one 7 years, $778.—*Atlanta American.*

Prices at Richmond, July 25: No. 1 men, 20 to 26 years old, from $1,450 to $1,500; best grown girls, 17 to 20 years old, from $1,275 to $1,325; girls from 15 to 17 years old, $1,150 to $1,250; girls from 12 to 15 years old, $1,000 to $1,100; best plough boys, 17 to 20 years old, $1,350 to $1,425; boys from 15 to 17 years old, $1,250 to $1,375; boys from 12 to 15 years old, $1,100 to $1,200.

Price of Slaves in Missouri.—At a sale of slaves that took place last Monday, says the St. Louis *Republican* of the 20th inst., at Bowling Green in this state, the following prices were obtained: Negro man, 50 years old, $845; do., 55, $795, negro woman, 60, $195; do., 40, 801; negro girl, 13, $1,187; do., 10, $900; do., 6, $535.

Note 26, *page* 36.

Adam de Marisco, a native of Somerset, England, was a Franciscan monk and a doctor at Oxford, and acquired such a great reputation in the thirteenth century, by his learning, as to be surnamed *Doctor Illustratus.* In Italy, he was on intimate terms with, and greatly esteemed by, St. Anthony of Padua, and in England much thought of by Robert Greathead, bishop of Lincoln, 1235–1254. He was named bishop of Ely circa 1256, but declined the dignity on learning that the pope had already nominated Hugh de Balsham to that see. He wrote on The Song of Songs; Questions of Theology; Paraphrases on St. Denis, the Areopagite; and died in, or about the year 1257.—*Moreri, Grand Dict.' Hist.; Luiscius, Algem. Wordenboek.*

Note 27, *page* 36.

Tamahican is a word common to most of the Algonquin dialects. Its root may perhaps be found in the verb *ehouen,* to strike, or knock.—*Mithridates,* III, iii, 354. "Tomahawk" is the Indian word anglicized.

Note 28, *Page* 36.

Henry Somerset, 1st Marquis of Worcester, was the son of Edward, 4th Earl of Somerset, to whose honors he succeeded in 1628. He was a nobleman of great piety and parts, and one of the richest of the English peers. He spent his fortune in the service of Charles I, for whom he defended the castle of Ragland against the rebels till the conclusion of the war, when it was surrendered on terms (August, 1646), which, however, were basely violated, and his lordship died a prisoner, in December of the same year. The Marquis of Worcester had early embraced the Catholic faith, and there appeared after his death, "Certamen Religiosum, or a Conference between King Charles I. and Henry late Marquis of Worcester, concerning religion;" "The Golden Apothegms of King Charles I. and Henry Marquis of Worcester." He was father of Edward, 2d Marquis of Worcester, famous for his connection with the discovery of the Power of Steam, and How to Sail against Wind and Tide, which Horace Walpole enumerates among "the amazing pieces of folly."—*Noble Authors*, p. 371, 378.

Note 29, *page* 37.

KINTAUKAUNS. Much ignorance prevails regarding the Indian *Kintacaws*. Some esteem them to have been debauched revels or bacchanalia, and hold them in horror, supposing them to be something akin to devil worship. Those who had the curiosity to investigate the matter, have given such accounts of the conduct of the Indians, on these occasions, as naturally lead to the conclusion that they paid a joint homage and supplication to some invisible being. The word is derived from the Delaware *Gentekehen*, to dance; and here it is supposed lies the key of the mystery. The Indians, it is well known, accompanied, if not celebrated, all their public acts or events by dances. Van der Donck, writing on the subject of the amusements of those people, says: "The old and middle aged conclude with smoking, and the young with a *kintacaw*." It was not restricted to any particular season of the year. During the Esopus war there was a *kintecaw* at the *Danskamer*, above Newburgh, in the month of August, "so that the woods rang again;" in another instance an Indian desired to be permitted to dance the *kintecaw*, before being put to death; and another having been led out to the place of execution, "danced the *kintekaye* all the way thither." The "Kintacaw," thus appears to have been simply a dance, which, however, received its character from the occasion on which it took place. It was a calumet *kintecaw* on concluding a peace or a treaty; a bear *kintecaw*, at the conclusion of a successful hunt of that animal; a war *kintecaw*, on the organization of an expedition against an enemy; and a death *kintecaw*, when the victim was led bleeding yet dancing to the stake.—*N. Y. Documentary History*, 8vo, IV, 63, 106; *Smith's History of New York*, Alb. ed., 76. See further, *Denton's Description of New York* (Gowans' ed.), p. 11, and *Carver's Travels*, London, 1778, p. 266, for particulars respecting the dances of the Indians.

Note 30, *page* 38.

KAKINDOWET—a Minister: from *Kakindowinin*, to teach, or preach to several persons.

Note 31, *page* 39.

THIS is a corruption of *Jubartes*, one of the names given to the humpbacked whales. Anderson, in his account of Iceland, gives it as *Jupiter fish*, and this has been erroneously supposed to be the derivation of the term. David Crantz, in his history of Greenland, furnishes the clue to its name, when he says of the Jupiter fish, that the "*Spanish whalers call it Gubartas, from an excrescence near the tail.*" Lacepede and Cuvier describe the *gibbar* and the *Jubarte.* Cuvier especially says that these names are given to them by the Basques. Now, *Jorobado* in Spanish means humpback, and its root is evidently the Latin *gibbus.*

The Basque whalers were the first to pursue the whale to its northern haunts, and in the beginning of the seventeenth century, when the Dutch and English took up the whaling business, the Basques were their instructors. This will account for the adoption of the word *jubarte* into the English and Dutch languages. See *Histoire des Peches*, vol. 1. Kline and other naturalists give the the coast of New England as its peculiar resort, and John Edward Gray, in his excellent catalogue of cetacea in the British Museum, gives the *Megaptera Americana*, or Bermuda humpback, which reaches a length of 88 feet, as the probable *Jubartes* of whalers.—*N. Y. Historical Magazine*, III, 52–3.

Note 32, *page* 40.

Sir THOMAS BROWNE, Kt., was born in London, 19th November, 1605. Having been educated near Winchester, he entered Pembroke college, Oxford, in the beginning of the year 1623, and having taken his degree in arts, proceeded to Leyden, where he was made Doctor of Medicine. He settled at Norwich, where he practised his profession for many years. His famous work, Religio Medici, was published in 1642. This was followed by Pseud. Epidem. Enquiries into very many received Tenents and commonly presumed Truths, or Enquiries into Common and Vulgar Errours; London, 1646; small folio. This work, which is still popular, has gone through many editions. Nature's Cabinet Unlocked; Urn Burial; the Garden of Cyrus, and a volume of Miscellanies, are also by the same author, who received the honor of knighthood in 1671, and died at Norwich in the year 1682. He was interred in St. Peter's church, where a monument was erected to his memory. A copy of the inscription on his monument is in *Wood's Athen. Oxon.* II, 536.

Note 33, *page* 41.

John Robinson was a merchant of New York as early as 1676, where he married Gritie, widow of Cornelis Dircksen. In 1678 he hired a dwelling house on the east side of the city "towards the fortification near the water portt," and purchased, in November, 1679, for £120, the Shottwell farm containing 38¼ acres of land. This farm was situate on the east side of the city, and was bounded on the S. W. by the land of John Bassett, and on the N. W. by John Young's land. It included a run of water called Saw-mill creek, and a leather mill which Shottwell had erected thereupon, also a pond of water ranging N. E. unto the woods 120 rods. On the first of January, 1680, Mr. Robinson sold one-half the Shottwell farm, mill and water privileges, to John Lewin and Robert Woolley, merchants of London, for the sum of £60, and the property passed subsequently into the hands of William Coxe, Robinson's partner in trade.—*N. Y. Book of Deeds*, V, 113, VI, 208, 414. Mr. Valentine's impression is, that this farm was on the west side of Pearl, and north of Pine street. Mr. William J. Davis, another well known antiquary of New York, adds: "In Common Council in 1680, a resolution was passed that the water lots between John Robinson's and William Beeckman's lands along the Smith's valley be sold at auction to pay some public assessments. (The Smith's valley extended from Cedar nearly to Beekman street.) The Damen farm adjoined Wall street on the north; next to which was Mrs. Tysen's, and John Robinson's land probably joined her's. Hence, I think it evident that the 'Orchard,' extended from about Cedar street to Maiden lane." Thereabouts, probably, in the heart of the Second ward of the city, was the scene of the Bear hunt referred to by Mr. Woolley. New York is still famous for hunting *Bears*, but the amusement has been transferred to a locality further to the south, and known by the name of Wall street. In the same vicinity the first Methodist church in the city was erected, and thereabouts, too, the late Washington Irving, whose death a nation still mourns, first saw the light of day.

Mr. Robinson was alderman for the West ward in 1683, 1684 and 1685, but did not decease in New York. Dirck van der Cliff, Robinson's brother in law, owned, east of the Shottwell farm, an orchard through which a street was afterwards run, and called Cliff street, after the said Dirck van der Cliff.

Note 34, *page* 42.

Elizabeth, daughter and coheir of Sir Robert Christopher, Knt., of Alford in Lincolnshire, married Bennett, second Lord Sherard on the Irish peerage, by whom she had one son and two daughters. One of these married Edward, Lord Viscount Irwin, and the other, the Duke of Rutland. She lost her husband in the year 1700. Her son Bennett succeeded to the title that year, and was created Lord Harborough in 1714, and Earl of Harborough in 1719. His lordship married Mary, daughter of Sir Henry Calverly.

Note 35, *page* 45.

ME-TA-OW. Bishop Baraga, in his *Dictionary of the Otchipwe Language*, says, *Midew* means an Indian of the order of the Grand Medicine, *Midewiwin* being the name of that order. And in the Rev. Mr. Dougherty's *Chippewa Primer*, p. 41, *Metawa* means—he dances (at a feast). As part of the Indian cure consists of the dancing of the physician, perhaps the root of the Indian word in the text may be thus arrived at.

Note 36, *Page* 47.

Captain JOHN MANNING came to New York with Governor Nicolls in 1664, and in September of that year accompanied Colonel Cartwright in his expedition for the reduction of Fort Orange, where he attended and was a witness to the first treaty which the English concluded with the Five Nations.—*N. Y. Gen. Ent.*, I, 42. After the surrender of the place he was left in charge of the fort (*Ibid.* 45), In 1667, he was appointed Sheriff of the city of New York (*Ord. War. and Letters.* II, 177, 188), and held that office until 1672 inclusive. In 1669 he was named a member of the commission sent the same year to the Esopus, to regulate the affairs of that district (*Ibid; Council Min.*, III, 12, 434, 530, 535); also, justice for the West Riding of Yorkshire, and acted as high Sheriff of Yorkshire from 1671 to 1673.—*Gen. Ent.*, IV, 201. During the administration of Colonel Lovelace, he seems to have been high in the confidence of that governor, of whose council he was a member, and who, whenever called by business to any distance from the city, always left Fort James and the public peace in charge of Captain Manning (see *Instruc.*, *ibid.*, 243). It was whilst charged with these duties in 1671, that an express arrived from Albany at New York with the fearful news of the approach of the French. Manning forthwith dispatched an express to Governor Lovelace, who was at Staten Island. Instead of approving his officer's activity, the latter was snubbed by the governor for his "impatience."—*Court of Assize Record*, 732. Whether discouraged by this reception or, as he himself admits, hopeless of making any effectual defence, he made no resistance when the wolf came actually, in 1673, in the shape of the Dutch, but unconditionally surrendered the country to them, and went back to England, where he arrived in January, 1674, his wife having died on the passage. He immediately waited on the King and the Duke of York and the principal officers of state, on which occasion the King gave it as his opinion that Fort James was not tenable. Captain Manning returned to New York in the Diamond frigate with Governor

Andros in 1674, and soon after was tried by court martial on charges of treachery and cowardice. He was acquitted of treachery, but found guilty of every other charge, and on 5th February, 1675, sentenced "to be carried back to prison and from thence brought out to the publick place before the City Hall, there to have his sword broken over his head, and from that time be rendered uncapable of wearing a Sword or serving his Majesty in any publick employ or place of benefitt and Trust within the Government."—*N. Y. Doc. Hist.*, 8vo, III, 80–100; *N. Y. Council Min.*, III, ii, 24. Thereupon he retired to his Island, where, according to Mr. Wooley's account, he does not seem to have permitted his disgrace to disturb his philosophy.

Manning's Island was called Minnahanock by the Indians;* Varken (or Hog) Island by the Dutch; it had been purchased originally by Governor Van Twiller in 1637, and granted in 1651 to Captain Francis Fyn, who figures in a lampoon against Governor Stuyvesant about that time (*O'Callaghan's New Netherland*, II, 181, 581). On the breaking out of the war against the Dutch in 1666, it was confiscated. On the 8th February, 1668, it was granted to Captain Manning, whereupon it passed by the name of "Manning's Island." On the 1st of August following, Captain Manning executed a deed conveying the island to Matthias Nicolls, *in trust*, for the use of the said Manning during his life, and after his decease for the use of his wife, if she should survive him, and after their decease, entailing it on Mary Manningham, daughter of Mrs. Manning by a former husband, and the heirs of her body, and for want of such heirs, after her death, to her brother Henry Manningham and his heirs.—*N. Y. Patents*, I, 99, 146. In 1676 (the year after Captain Manning was "broke"), the above named Mary Manningham married Robert Blackwell, "late of Elizabethtown, in New Jersey, merchant" (*N. Y. Deed Book*, I, 130); the property in consequence was, after Captain Manning's death, called "*Blackwell's Island*," which name it bears at present. It is now the property of the city of New York, and is occupied by a Penitentiary, Alms House, Lunatic Asylum, Hospital, and similar institutions. It contains 120 acres, and cost the city of New York $50,000. The date of Captain Manning's death is not ascertained. He seems, however, to have been alive in 1686, when there was some difficulty between him and Mrs. Blackwell respecting the island, and she entered a caveat against the issuing of any patent to him for it, for a longer term than his life.

Note 37, *page* 48.

Henry Hammond, D. D., was born on 26th August, 1605, in Surrey, England. His father was physician to the Prince Henry, son of James I, after whom he was called. Having gone through his studies at Eton and Oxford, he devoted

* Minnahanock is derived from the Mohegan word *Minauhan*, an island, and *uck*, a termination signifying locality, and means literally, "At the Island."

himself to the study of theology, and received holy orders in 1629, and in 1633 was appointed rector of Penhurst, Kent. In 1643, he was made archdeacon of Chichester, but on the breaking out of the civil war, he became obnoxious to the party in the ascendant, on account of his attachment to his sovereign, and was obliged to remain concealed for several years, during which he composed various works in English and Latin; these were afterwards published in London, 4 vols. folio. His principal works are: Practical Catechism, or Abridgment of Christian Morals; Notes on the New Testament and on the Psalms. M. le Clerc wrote a criticism on some of these notes. When Charles II. was about to be recalled, Dr. Hammond was placed in charge of the diocese of Worcester, of which see he, without doubt, would have been appointed bishop, had he lived; but his life was unfortunately cut short on the 25th April, 1660, in the 55th year of his age.

Note 38, *page* 49.

Ancient Funeral Customs.—The following is copied from a memoir read by Judge Benson before the New York Historical Society in 1816: "A family in Albany, and from the earliest time, of the name of Wyngaard. The last, in the male line, Lucas Wyngaard, died about sixty years ago, never married, and leaving estate: the invitation to his funeral very general. Those who attended, returned after the interment, as was the usage, to the house of the deceased at the close of the one day, and a number never left it until the dawn of the next. In the course of the night a pipe of wine, stored in the cellar for some years before for the occasion, drank; dozens of papers of tobacco consumed; grosses of pipes broken: scarce a whole decanter or glass left; and, to crown it, the pall-bearers made a bonefire of their scarves on the hearth."

When Philip Livingston of New York died in 1749, his funeral expenses amounted to the sum of five hundred pounds, or $1,250. On that occasion two ceremonies were performed; one at his manor among his tenantry, and one at his residence in New York. At each place a pipe of wine was spiced for the guests. The bearers at the several places were presented with mourning rings, silk scarfs and handkerchiefs. The eight bearers in New York had each a gift of a monkey spoon (that is having a monkey carved on the handle), and at the manor *all* the tenantry had a gift of a pair of black gloves and a handkerchief. In a later period Gov. Wm. Livingston wrote in the Independent Reflector of 1753, his objections to extravagance in funerals, and his wife, it was said, was the first who ventured as an example of economy, to substitute linen scarfs for the former silk ones.—*Watson's Olden Times of New York*, 308. These customs continued down to a late period. Professor Morse writing in 1789, says: Their funeral ceremonies are equally singular. None attend them without a previous invitation. At the appointed hour they meet at the neighboring houses or stoops, until the corpse is brought out. Ten or twelve persons are appointed to take the bier all together, and are not relieved. The clerk then desires the gentlemen (for ladies never walk to the grave, nor even attend the funeral, unless of a near relation) to fall into the procession. They go to the grave, and return to the house of mourning in the same order. Here the tables are handsomely set and furnished with cold and spiced wine, tobacco and pipes, and candles, paper, &c., to light them. The conversation turns upon promiscuous subjects.—*Munsell's Annals of Albany*, I, 315.

Robert Townsend, Esq., of Albany, informs us, that he was told by his mother, recently deceased, that a similar custom was observed as late as 1810, after the interment of General Ten Broeck, one of the most respectable citizens of the state of New York. Those invited to the funeral returned to the family mansion, where a cask of Madeira which had been stowed away by the old gentleman many years before, was, in accordance with the ancient usage, broached for the guests; and several hogsheads of Beer were rolled out on the lawn in front of the house for the free use of all comers. It is only proper to add, that this singular custom died out with the last generation.

Note 39, *page* 51.

This is a Narragansett word. "After harvest, after hunting, when they enjoy a calm of peace, health, plenty, prosperity, then the Indians have *Nickommo*, a feast, especially in winter. He or she who maketh this *Nickommo*, feast or dance, besides the feasting, of sometimes twenty, fifty, an hundred, yea, I have seen near a thousand persons at one of these feasts,—give a great quantity of money, and all sorts of their goods, according to and sometimes beyond their estate, in several small parcels of goods or money, to the value of eighteen pence, two shillings, or thereabouts, to one person; and that person that receives this gift, upon the receiving it, goes out, and hollows thrice for the health and prosperity of the party that gave it, the master or mistress of the feast. By this feasting and gifts, the devil drives on their worships pleasantly (as he doth all false worships, by such plausible earthly arguments of uniformities, universalities, antiquities, immunities, dignities, rewards unto submitters, and the contrary to refusers) so that they run far and near and ask, *Awaun Nickommit*, Who makes the feast?"—*Roger Williams' Key unto the Language of the Indians of New England.*

Note 40, *page* 52.

Nut signifies "Belly" in the Etchemin dialect; *Notasung* is the corresponding Delaware word; *Nutah*, the Nanticoke. Reference is made to these *Notas*, or *Denotas*, by Van der Donck in the "Great Remonstrance of New Netherland," where they are described as Bags wherewith the Indians measured their corn.—*N. Y. Colonial Documents*, I, 281.

Note 41, *page* 53.

WASS-RA-NEK signifies a Torch; the Algonkin word for Light is, *Waselenican.* DU PONCEAU, *Mem. sur les Langues Indiennes*, p. 265; from *Washsayah*, or *Wacheyek*, the light.—*Dougherty's Chippewa Primer*, p. 47.

Note 42, *page* 54.

THE reader is referred to "Denton's Brief Description of New York:" Gowans, 1845, p. 36, for further particulars respecting the Long Island Indians.

Note 43, *page* 57.

WILHELMUS VAN NIEUWENHUYZEN. The Reformed Dutch church of the city of New York being, in consequence of the incapacity of the Rev. Mr. Drisius, wholly destitute of a minister in 1670, an invitation, or call, was sent to Holland for a clergyman, with a guarantee from Governor Lovelace that he should receive an annual salary of 1000 guilders, equal to $400, with a house free of rent, and firewood without charge.—*N. Y. Col. Doc.*, III, 189. The Rev. Mr Nieuwenhuyzen came, in consequence, to New York in the course of the summer of 1671, as colleague to the Rev. Mr. Drisius, who dying in 1672, Mr. Van Nieuwenhuyzen succeeded as sole minister to the church, being the seventh in succession from the Rev. Mr. Michaëlius. A few years after, namely in 1675, he had a difficulty with the Rev. Nicholas Van Renselaer, a minister of Albany, who, he asserted, "aloude in ye street," was not "a Lawfull minister nor his admittance at Albany lawfull;" maintaining "afterwards at Mr. Ebbing's, one of the elders," that no one having orders from the Church of England had sufficient authority to be admitted to administer the sacraments (Mr. Van Renselaer having received holy orders from the Rt. Rev. John Earle, Bishop of Salisbury, 1663–1665). The matter begat such excitement that it was brought before the governor and council on the 25th September. On that occasion, Mr. Van Renselaer exhibited proofs of his having been chaplain to the Dutch ambassador at London, and afterwards minister to the Dutch church at Westminster, and lecturer at St. Margaretts Loathbury, London. Mr. Van Nieuwenhuyzen was thereupon called on to declare whether a minister ordained in England by a bishop, be not qualified to administer the sacraments. The consideration of the case was resumed by the council on the 30th, when Jeronimus Ebbing and Peter Stoutenburg, elders; Jacob Teunisse Kay, Reyneer Willemse, Gerritt Van Tright, Isaac Van Vleck, deacons of the church at New York, appeared with their minister before the board. Mr. Van Nieuwenhuyzen "rather justified himself in his answer;" but he and his church officers finally considered it most prudent to yield to Governor Andros, and to admit, "That a Minister ordayned in England by the Bishops is every way capable, &c."—*N. Y. Council Min.*, III, 54–59. Smith in his *History of New York*, erroneously calls this clergyman, "Niewenhyt, minister of the church at Albany," and then draws equally erroneous references from the dispute above referred to. Gideon Schaets was minister of the Reformed Dutch church at Albany at the time and for several years after.—*N. Y. Doc. Hist.*, 8vo, III, 878. Equally erroneous is another statement, that Mr. Van Nieuwenhuyzen retired to Brooklyn in 1676. Mr. Van Nieuwenhuyzen continued in charge at New York until his death, which took place in that city on the 17th February, 1681. Annekie Mauritz, his widow, survived him. It is clear, from the evidence of Mr. Wooley, that Mr. Van Nieuwenhuyzen was an accomplished scholar, whilst from the same evidence it is also clear, that in his ministry he sometimes exhibited more zeal than charity.

Note 44, page 57.

Lord George Russell was the youngest son of William 5th Earl and 1st Duke of Bedford, and brother of the celebrated Lord William Russell who was beheaded in 1683. He was graduated at Magdalen college, Oxford, on the 4th February, 1666–7, when he was created Master of Arts. After making the tour of Europe he entered the army, and came to America. He was in Boston, and presented with the freedom of that city in 1680, as we find by the following entry in the Records: "4th February, 1679–80. It is ordered that the hon. George Russell, Esq., now resident with us in Boston, be admitted to the freedom of the corporation, if he please to accept thereof." He accepted of it and took the oath 13th February following, before the governor and assistants. He was in garrison as an ensign, at Albany, about the year 1687, and in the city of New York in 1689; when Captain Baxter and he being "known to be Roman Catholicx, were for that reason by the Lt. Gov. [Nicholson] and Council to avoid all jealousies, sent not only out of the garrisons, but even out of the Province." He married Mary, daughter and heir of Mr. Pendleten; and died in the year 1692, leaving issue one son, who died unmarried.—*Wiffen's Hist. of the House of Russell*, II, 223, 224; *Brydges' Collins*, sub titulo "Bedford;" *Rec. of the Col. of the Mass. Bay*, V, 264; *Hutchinson's Hist. of Mass.*, Salem ed., I, 299; *N. Y. Col. Doc.*, III, 640, IV, 132; *N. Y. Council Min.*, IV, 54.

Note 45, page 58.

Frederick Philipse is said to have been a native of East Friesland. He was born in the year 1625, and immigrated to New Netherland about the year 1658, being by trade a carpenter. After his arrival here, he was employed in that capacity for some time in the public service, both at Bergen and at Esopus. In 1660 he embarked in trade, as appears by the public Records:

"20th Sept., 1660. It being proposed in Council by the Hon[ble] Director General on behalf of Frederick Philipsen, his Honor's late carpenter, that said Frederick Philipsen is disposed to make a voyage to Virginia with some merchandize, if the company's sloop be hired to him, &c."—*N. Y. Col. MSS.*, XI, 416; *Alb. Rec.*, XIV, 69; XXIV, 415.

A few years after this he married Margaret Hardenbroeck, the widow of Peter Rudolfus, a woman who was an active trader among the Indians; with whom he acquired some property, which may be said to have laid the foundation of his fortune;* for he soon became the wealthiest merchant in New York. He was appointed one of the aldermen of that city in 1675, and in September of the same year was sworn one of the council of Governor Andros. He continued to hold a seat in that body twenty-three years, with the exception of the brief administration of Jacob Leisler, which he opposed. When Kidd and Red sea pirates flourished in New York, Frederick Philipse became implicated like many others, in that illegal trade, and was censured by the authorities in England. Finding himself in bad odor, he resigned his seat in the council in 1698. Mr. Philipse acquired large tracts of land in Westchester county, N. Y., which were erected in the year 1693, into the manor of Philipsborough, where he was buried in 1702, in the 78th year of his age. His second wife was Catherine Van Cortland, widow of John Dervall.

Note 46, *page* 60.

Skating Grounds of New York.—Skating has been always a favorite exercise in New York, though we must say, that men and women are no longer seen "as it were flying upon their skates from place to place with marketing upon their Heads and Backs." The Kolck or Collect, a sheet of fresh water which covered the ground now occupied by the halls of justice in Centre street, and all that neighborhood, communicated in ancient times with Lespinard's pond and meadows, lying between North Moore and Green street, near the west end of what is at present Canal street. This was the great skating ground of the last century, where the gallants of the hour displayed, as a quaint writer expresses it, "theire graceful caracoles and pirouettes," ever and anon skimming at pleasure from one collection of water to the other, under the bridge which connected upper with lower Broadway. There William the fourth, late King of England, might be seen when "*a Middy*," attached to the flag ship of Rear-Admiral Digby, attended by superior officers, trying his "tacks" on the slippery ice, in the winter of 1781-2. Tradition hath it, that a stratagem had been planned by certain of Washington's men to capture this royal scion of the house of Hanover, and thereby secure a valuable prize, while enjoying himself

* The marriage contract between these parties is on record in the Minutes of the Orphan Court, City Hall, New York. The published pedigree of the family is incorrect, in many particulars, as regards its founder in America.

in his healthful exercise on the Collect pond. It is further said that the project had well nigh succeeded. Seemingly in anticipation of that success, one of the American papers wrote: "The boy William Henry Guelph, lately arrived at New York, will perhaps soon be in our power. In that event we shall not visit the sins of the father on the child, but send him home to his mother."

But those times have passed away, and not a pair of those feet which now daily promenade, in patent leather boots, past the Hospital at the head of Pearl street, has ever skated on the Collect or Lespinard's meadows. I have myself, adds Mr. Gowans, seen people skating between Washington market and Jersey city. To the spectators on shore, the skaters whilst whirling about on the river, did not appear larger than a good sized turkey in the act of flapping his wings; and I have heard that journeys have been performed on skates between New York and Albany.

Modern improvements have driven skating "out of town." When we were lads, says the editor of the *N. Y. Times* and *Messenger*, the nearest skating pond was on Stuyvesant's meadows, which then lay east of the Third avenue, and spread away from Eighth street to the river. Next to these, but further out, was Cato's pond, nearly up to the old shot-tower. These were fine large skating ponds in our eyes, but so terribly far away, that we made our preparations for going to them as if for a serious journey. Our pet place, however, was smaller, but handier. It was a pond at the corner of Thirteenth street and Broadway, nearly a square large. A block and pump maker's shanty, built on piles, stood in one edge of it. Why it was built there, we have, in youth, often endeavored to imagine, and after much patience of philosophising, came to the conclusion that it was for convenience, and to try whether his pumps would draw water before he sent them away to be put down in the old-fashioned wells at the street corners.

Accommodation for skaters is, we are happy to record the fact, now provided at the public expense. A skating pond of about twenty acres large, admirably planned for comfort and adapted for the purpose, has been laid out in the Central Park, where young men have an opportunity of indulging in this healthy exercise free from danger. Instead of trudging away on foot for miles, as their fathers had to do to get at the skating place, the youth of the present day have but to step into one of the avenue cars and bowl off to the Central Park, strap their skates, and cut carlicues till their young legs have had enough of it.

But don't let those merry scamps of boys altogether monopolize the fun. Let the girls mount the swift skate also. It is just as healthy for them; and what a charming thing it will be to see five hundred cherry-cheeked, healthy beauties—goddesses in crinoline and mortals in plumptitudinous loveliness—gliding, whirling, and now and then sitting down, without exactly intending it, on the slippery ice. Let the ladies patronise the Central Park skating pond. They can make themselves adorable enough in Polish skating costume, to drive all the men and boys in New York mad as March hares. Let them remember, too, that the police arrangements for order, propriety and comfort at the pond, are perfect, and a lady can enjoy herself there with as absolute comfort as at the opera.

Note 47, *page* 61.

George Heathcote, the Quaker captain. The earliest instance that we find on record of a Quaker commanding a ship is in *N. Y. Col. Documents*, II, 461, where it stated that such a vessel arrived in the port of New Amsterdam on the 20th October, 1661, and refused to "strike to the port, being a quaker." The ship mentioned in the text was the *Hopewell*. She was commanded by George Heathcot "of Rattilife in the county of Middlesex, Eng." (*N. Y. Deed Book*, IV, 349), a sturdy Quaker, who "on the first of the sixth month 1672," being owner and commander of a ship, was imprisoned by Governor Bellingham of Massachusetts, "for delivering him a letter and not putting of his hat."—*Besse's Sufferings of the Quakers*, II, 259. Not encouraged by this reception, he seems to have subsequently turned his face to New York, from which port he sailed for England in August, 1675.—*N. Y. Council Min.*, III, part ii, 46. He returned the following year, having chartered the ship John and Mary of Weymouth, and purchased land in New York "above the smith's garden," through which a street 28 feet wide was ordered to be opened in 1686.—*N. Y. Council Min.*, V, 146, 151. He was master of "the pink Hopewell" in 1679, which vessel cleared for London, July 17, 1680 (*Orders and Warrants*, XXXII, 21, 26, 94); and in this voyage it was that he was accompanied by the Rev. Mr. Wooley. The pink Hopewell, George Heathcote, master, cleared from New York again for London, 23d June, 1681 (*N. Y. Pass Book*, p. 4), on which occasion he carried William Dyre, the collector of New York, a prisoner to England by order of the Court of Assize. Besse says, George Heathcot was fined in London in 1683 for refusing to bear arms.—*Opus sup. cit.*, I, 462. We find him again in New York in 1685, in 1688, and in 1691. In 1688 he was master of the ship Yorke.—*N. Y. Deed Book*, VIII, 208. He subsequently settled in Bucks county, Penn. It has been stated that he died unmarried in New York in 1685; but this is clearly erroneous. Mr. Heathcote married the daughter of Samuel Groom of New Jersey.—*N. Y. Council Min.*, V, 71. His daughter married John Barber of London; he had two sisters, one of whom was Mrs. Hannah Browne, and the other, Mrs. Anne Lupton; and he died in November, 1710. By his will on file in the Surrogate's office New York, and bearing date 14th November, and proved 24th November of that year, he liberates his three negro slaves, gives 500 acres of land near Shrewsbury, N. J., to Thomas Carlton, to be called Carlton settlement, and constitutes his "cozen Caleb Heathcote," residuary legatee.

1860.] [No. 19.

GOWANS.

CATALOGUE OF

Ancient and Rare American Books,

FOR SALE AT THE AFFIXED PRICES,

STORE—81, 83 and 85 CENTRE STREET, NEW YORK,

(*Two Blocks East of Broadway.*)

CATALOGUES SENT GRATIS TO ANY PART OF THE UNITED STATES.

" Give me leave
To enjoy myself: that place that does contain
My BOOKS, *the best companions, is to me*
A glorious court, where hourly I converse
With the old sages and philosophers;
And sometimes, for variety, I confer
With kings and emperors, and weigh their counsels;
Calling their victories, if unjustly got,
Unto a strict account, and, in my fancy,
Deface their ill-placed statues. Can I then
Part with such constant pleasures, to embrace
Uncertain vanities? No! be it your care
To augment a heap of wealth; it shall be mine
To increase in knowledge by these means."—J. FLETCHER.

" If the price of old books anent America whether native or foreign should continue to augment in value in the same ratio as they have done for the last thirty years, their prices must become fabulous, or rather like the books of the Sibyls, rise above all valuation. In the early part of the present century, the Bay Hymn Book (the first book printed in North America), then an exceedingly rare book, no one would have supposed would bring one hundred dollars; now, a copy was lately sold for nearly six hundred, and a perfect copy at this time would bring one thousand. Elliott's Grammar of the Indian Tongues was lately sold for $100, *a small tract. The author's version of the Scriptures into the Indian Language could be purchased fifty years ago for* $50, *now it is worth* $500; *Cotton Mather's Magnalia Christi Americana,* $6 *was then thought a good price, now* $50 *is thought cheap for a good copy; Smith's History of Virginia* $30, *now* $75; *Stith's History of Virginia, then* $5, *now* $20; *Smith's History of New Jersey, then* $2, *now* $20; *Thomas's History of Printing, then* $2, *now* $15; *Denton's History of New Netherlands,* $5, *now* $50. *These are but a few out of many hundreds that could be named that have risen from trifling to extraordinary prices, in the short space of half a century."*

.... Western Memorabilia

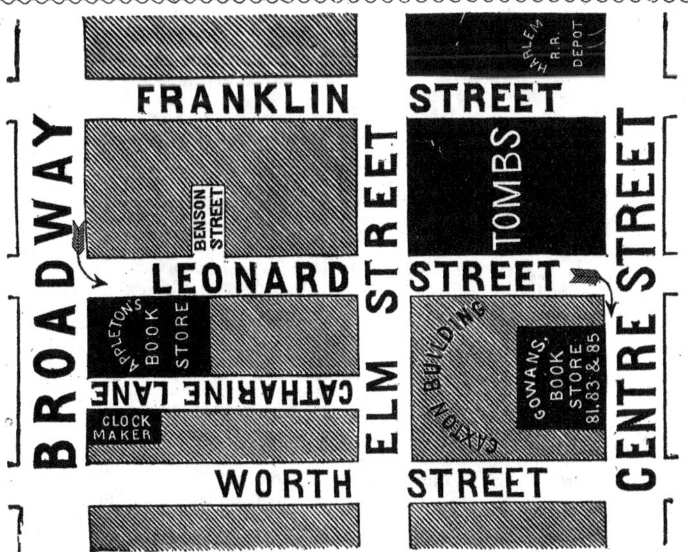

ACOSTA, JOSEPH. Histoire Naturelle et moralle des Indes, tant Orientalles qu' Occidentalles: Ou, il est traicté des choses remarquables du Ciel, des Elemens, Metaux, Plantes et Animaux qui sont propres de ce pays. Ensemble des mœurs, ceremonies, loix, governemens and guerres des mesmes Indiens. 12mo. pp. 798. $5 00. Paris, 1600.

ACOSTA, JOSEPH. The Naturall and Morall Historie of the East and West Indies. Intreating of the remarkeable things of Heaven, of the Elements, Mettalls, Plants and Beasts which are proper to that country: together with the Manners, Ceremonies, Lawes, Governements and Warres of the Indians. Written in Spanish by J. A., and translated into English by E. G. 4to. pp. 604. $15 00. London, 1604.

ADAMS, C. B. Catalogue of Shells collected at Panama, with Notes of their Synonymy, Station and Geographical Distribution. 8vo. pp. 342. (*privately printed.*) $5 00. New York, 1852.

ADAMS, JOHN. Twenty-Six Letters upon interesting subjects, respecting the Revolution of America. Written in Holland in the year 1780, &c. 12mo, pr. pp. 64. $2 25. New York, 1789.

ADAMS, JOHN Q. Report upon Weights and Measures. Prepared by order of Congress. 8vo. pp. 248. $5 00. Washington, 1821.

ADYE, STEPHEN PAYNE. A Treatise in Courts Martial. Containing: I. Remarks on Martial Law and Courts Martial in general. II. The Manner of proceeding against offenders. To which is added, An Essay on Military Punishments and Rewards. 12mo. pp. 146. $5 00. New York, 1769.

ALBANY. Laws and Ordinances, of the Mayor, Recorder, Alderman, and Commonalty of the city of Albany. 4to. pp. 66. $6 50. Albany, 1773.

ALEXANDER, EARL OF STIRLING AND DEVON. Vindication of the Rights and Titles, Political and Territoriel, as Lord Proprietor of Canada and Nova-Scotia. By John L. Hayes. Also the Trial of Lord Stirling, being Part II of the Vindication of the Rights and Titles, Political and Territoriel, of Alexander, Earl of Stirling and Devon, Hereditary Lieutenant-General and Lord Proprietor of Canada Nova-Scotia. By John L. Hays. (*curious fac-simile of the original grant.*) 8vo. pp. 52 and 76. $5 00. Washington, 1853.

ALEXANDER AND RUFUS, or a Series of Dialogues on Church Communion, in two parts. The first, being a vindication of Scriptural Church Communion in opposition to Latitudinarian schemes. The second, being a Defence of the Communion maintained in the Secession Church. 8vo. pp. 461. $3 00. Pittsburgh, 1820.

ALLEN, WILLIAM. An Address delivered at Northampton, Mass., on the evening of October 29, 1854, in commemoration of the close of the Second Century, since the settlement of the town. 8vo. pp. 56. $1 00. Northampton, 1855.

AMERICA, CONSTITUTIONS of the several Independent States of; The Declaration of Independence; The Articles of Confederation between said States; The Treatise between his most Christian Majesty and the United States of America. Published by order of Congress, 1782. The Rights of Great Britain asserted against the Claims of America; being an answer to the Declaration of the General Congress. The ninth Edition to which is now added a further Refutation of Dr. Price's state of the National Department. A Declaration of the Representatives of the Colonies of North America, now met in General Congress. Articles of Confederation and perpetual Union by the Colonies. A Refutation of Dr. Price, &c., &c., all in one vol. 8vo. Calf. $5 00. London, 1776–82.

AMERICAN. Dialogues of the American Dead. 8vo. pp. 43. $1 00. Philadelphia, 1814.

The interlocutors in these Dialogues, are Washington, Alfred, William Tell, Hamilton and Fisher Ames.

AMERICAN ETHNOLOGICAL SOCIETY, Transactions of. 2 vols. 8vo. pp. 505, 637. Maps. $5 00. New York, 1845–48.

AMERICAN REGISTER, The, or General Repository of History, Politics, and Science, from 1806 to 1810. 7 vols. 8vo. $8 50. Philadelphia, 1807.

AMERICAN STATE PAPERS. Documents, Legislative and Executive, of the Congress of the United States, from the first Session commencing March 3, 1789, to March 3, 1823. Selected and edited under the authority of Congress by *Walter Lowrie*, Secretary of the Senate, and Matthew St. Clare Clark, Clerk of the House of Representatives. 21 vols. Fol. Half bound in Russia. $250 00. Washington, 1832–34.

This publication is classified as follows, namely: Vols. 1, 2, 3, 4, *Foreign Relations;* 5, 6, *Indian Affairs;* 7, 8, 9, *Finance;* 10, 11, *Commerce and Navigation;* 12, 13, *Military Affairs;* 14, *Naval Affairs;* 15, *Post Office;* 16, 17, 18, *Public Lands;* 19, *Claims;* 20 *and* 21, *Miscellanies.*

AMERIGO VESPUCCI. Elogio che ha riportato il premio Dalla Nobile Accademia etrusca Di Cortona, Nel di 15, Ottobre dell' anno 1788. Con una dissertazione Giustification di questo celebre Navigatore del P. Stanislao, lanovai delle scuole pie pubblico professere di fisica-matematica. Terza Edizione con Illustrazione ed Aggiunte, e con una Seconda Dissertazione sulle Vicende delle Longitudini Geograsiche. 4to. pp. 75. $2 00. 1790.

A SERMON, Preached at the Consecration of the Right Reverend Dr. Samuel Seabury, Bishop of the Episcopal Church in Connecticut. By a Bishop of the Episcopal Church of Scotland. 8vo. pp. 50. $1 50. Rare. Aberdeen, 1785.

ASHLEY, JOHN. Memoirs and Considerations concerning the Trade and Revenues of the British Colonies in America, with proposals for rendering these Colonies more beneficial to Great Britain. 8vo. pp. 160. H'lf bd. $3. London, 1740.

ARISTIDES. Essays on the spirit of Jacksonism, as exemplified in its deadly hostility to the Bank of the United States, and in the odious calumnies employed for its destruction. 8vo. pp. 151. $5. Philadelphia, 1835.

The Essays by Aristides are a collection of violent, perhaps truthful and consciencious attacks on General Jackson, but more especially on the incessant and unrelenting war he waged against the United States Bank. But it would appear that the performance did not convert the old hero, for he persecuted that institution till he finally overturned it, and with its fall thousands were ruined by consequence of having their all invested in it. When in full blast and good credit the shares sold for $125.00, *and when wound up* $1.50. *The author of this pungent treatise was Col. Thomas L. McKinney, well known as an author of aboriginal history, biography and antiquities, and his connection with General Cass during his governorship of the north-western territory, and their tour throughout the same; as well as with the Indian department at the seat of Government. He evidently had a very bad opinion of General Jackson, whom he knew intimately. He characterises him as possessing few or no virtues and stained with almost every negative and many positive vices. He was the greatest despot that ever wielded power; ignorant, proud, obstinate, head-strong, wilful, jealous, deceitful, implacable, unforgiving, vindictive, and ferociously revengful, at once the dupe and head of a hollow-hearted and domineering party. He, Col. McKinney, was an amiable, genial, warm-hearted man, often generous to his own injury. In conversation he was profuse in anecdote, historical, biographical and miscellaneous. In personal appearance he was tall, and erect in gait as a West Point cadet; florid complexion, and a physiogonomy resembling Julius Cæsar; his hair white and glistening as threads of silver; in short he was the perfect type of a noble-looking old soldier.*

He died in the spring of 1859, *after a sickness of not more than three or four days, of erysipelas, and what is remarkable not a single paper in the city of New York noticed the death of a man who had done much meritorious service for his country both as a soldier and an author. Thus verifying the old adage, " Out of sight, out of mind." Had he been in office his death and biography would have been sounded from north to south and from New York to California, but he had long since retired from public life into the shade of retirement. Hence this neglect.*

.... Western Memorabilia.

BAYLEY, RICHARD. An Account of the Epidemic Fever which prevailed in the city of New York, during part of the Summer and Fall of 1795. 8vo. Calf. pp. 160. $2 50 New York, 1796.

BERKSHIRE JUBILEE, Celebrated at Pittsfield, Mass., Aug. 22 and 23, 1844. 8vo. pp. 244. 8 plates. $1. Albany, 1845.

Contents.—Sermon by Mark Hopkins. A Poem by William Allen. Oration by Joshua Spencer. Recollections of Berkshire Indians, by Thomas Allen. Literature of Berkshire. Names of the Emigrant Sons of Berkshire. Besides many minor pieces in both prose and poetry.

BLAIR, JAMES (OF VIRGINIA). Our Savior's Divine Sermons on the Mount Explained in divers Sermons and Discourses. 4 vols. 7vo. Calf, neat. $10. London, 1740.

"—— *our author has, in my opinion, very aptly joined the* Commentator, Preacher, *and* Casuist, *all in one . . . . . . how happy a talent the author had in deciding points of great moment, in a very* few *and* plain *words, but the result of* deep consideration, *and discovering a great* compass of thought."—Dr. Waterland.

BONAPARTE, CHARLES LUCIAN. A Geographical and Comparative List of the Birds of Europe and North America. 8vo. pp. 67. $2 00. London, 1838.

BRADAEN, LOUIS. The Early Peopling of America, and its Discovery before the time of Columbus. 12mo. pp. 48. $1 50. New York, 1847.

BRITISH SPY. The Letters of the. Originally published in the Virginia Argus, in August and September, 1803. Third edition. 18mo. pp. 128. $1 50. Richmond, 1805.

BROWN, CHARLES B. Wieland the Transformer. An American Tale. 12mo. pp. 298. (Original edition.) $2 00. New York, 1798.

BUCANIERS. The History of the Bucaniers of America. 2 vols. 18mo. $4 00. London, 1774.

BUNGAY GEORGE W. Crayon Sketches and Off-hand Takings, Distinguished American Statesmen, Orators, Divines, Essayists, Editors, Poets, and Philanthropists. 12mo. pp. 156. 75 cts. Boston, 1852.

BUNYAN JOHN. The Pilgrims' Progress from this World to that which is to come. *With remarkable engravings.* 18mo. pp. 166. $3 50. Boston, 1744.

This is without doubt the first American edition of the world renowned " Pilgrims's progress," and the engravings must be amongst the first, if not the very first specimen of American engraving.

BUSHNELL, CHARLES I. An Arrangement of Tradesmen's Cards, Political Tokens, also, Election Medals, Medalets, &c., current in the United States of America for the last sixty years, described from the originals, chiefly in the collection of the author. With Engravings. 8vo. pp. 118. $3 00. New York, 1858.

CAMPBELL, A. A Connected View of the Principles and Rules by which the Living Oracles may be intelligibly and certainly interpreted; of the foundation on which all Christians may form one Communion; and of the Capital Positions sustained in the attempt to restore the Original Gospel and order of things; containing the Principal Extras of the Millennial Harbinger, revised and corrected. 12mo. pp. 408. $1.50. Bethany, Va., 1835.

CARTER, ST. LEGER L. Nugæ, by Nugator, or Pieces in Prose and Verse. 18mo. pp. 215. $1 25. Baltimore, 1844.

The above volume contains several ingenious parodies on well known English poems, a poem on tobacco, one on the battle of New Orleans, and several describing local scenes in Virginia; besides several prose pieces, biographical, critical, and historical.

CATALOGUES. Bibliothecæ Harvardianæ Cantabrigiæ Nov-Anglorum. 8vo. pp. 358. $2 00. Bostoniæ, 1790.

CENSUS. Aggregate amount of each description of Persons in the United States and their territories, according to the Census of 1820. 8vo. pp. 49. $1 00. 1820.

CENSUS. (The Fifth U. S. Census.) Or Enumeration of the Inhabitants of the United States, 1830. To which is prefixed a Schedule of the whole number of Persons within the several Districts of the United States, taken according to the Acts of 1790, 1800, 1810, 1820. Published by authority of an act of Congress. Folio. $3 50. Washington, 1832.

CENSUS U. S. Statistical View of the Population of the, from 1790 to 1830, inclusive. Furnished by the Department of State, in accordance with Resolutions of of the Senate of the United States on the 26th of February, 1833, and 31st of March, 1834. Folio. pp. 216. $2 00. Washington, 1835.

CENSUS. (The Sixth U. S.) Or Enumeration of the Inhabitants of the United States, as corrected at the Department of State, in 1840. Folio. $3 50. Washington, 1841.

CENSUS of the State of New York, for 1835. Containing an Enumeration of the Inhabitants of the State, with other Statistical Information, in pursuance of Chapter 3d of the first part of the Revised Statutes, and of the Act amending the same, passed on the 16th March, 1835. Folio. $2 00. Albany, 1836.

CENSUS (U. S.). The Seventh. 4to. pp. 1158. Half bound in russia. $6 00. Washington, 1832.

CENSUS of the State of New York for 1845. Containing an Enumeration of the Inhabitants of the State, with some other Statistical Information, in pursuance of Chapter 3d of the first part of the Revised Statutes, and of the Act amending the same, passed on the 7th of May, 1845. Folio. $3 00. Albany, 1846.

CENSUS of the State of New York for 1855. Prepared from the Original Returns, by Franklin B. Hough. Folio. pp. 597. $3 00. Albany, 1857.

CENTRAL AMERICA. Brief Statement, supported by Original Documents, of the Important Grants conceded to the Eastern Coast of Central America, Commercial and Agricultural Company, by the State of Guatemala With a Map of the Territory of Vera Paz, and another of the Port of San Tomas. 8vo. pp. 137. 2 maps. $2 00. London, 1839.

CHILDS. (Sir Joshua.) New Discourse on Trade, wherein is recommended several weighty points relating to Companies of Merchants, Navigation, Woollen Manufactures, Nature of Plantations, &c. Small 8vo. Bound. $5 00. 1694.

The author speaks thus of the early settlers of the North American Colonies: "New England, originally inhabited and since replenished by a sort of people called Puritans, Virginia and Barbadoe first peopled by a sort of loose vagrant people, vicious, and destitute of means to live." Newfoundland, Jamaica, &c., are treated on in a like manner.

CHRONICLES OF TURKEYTOWN, or the Works of Jeremy Peters. Containing the History of a Dreadful Catastrophe and Amours of Dr. Potts and Mrs. Peweetle, and the History of a Tatterdemalion. 12mo. pp. 238. $1 25. Philadelphia, 1829.

CLARK, PETER. A Defense of the Divine Right of Infant Baptism, being in reply to Dr. John Gills' book entitled, The Divine Right of Infant Baptism Examined and Disproved. 8vo. pp. 464. $3 00. Boston, N. E., 1752.

CLAYTON, JOHANNES. Flora Virginica Exhibens Plantas. Qua. V. C. Ed. Joh. Frea Gronoveus. 8vo. $5 00. Lugduni, 1739.

*** *This is the first treatise on botany written in America.*

CLINTON, SIR HENRY. An Answer to the part of the Narrative which relates to Earl Cornwallis' campaign during the war of North America. 8vo. pp. 268. Uncut. $2 00. London, 1783.

COBBETT, WILLIAM. The Life of Thomas Paine, interspersed with Remarks and Reflections. By Peter Porcupine. 12mo. pp. 60. $2 00. Philadelphia, 1797.

COLCROFT, HENRY ROEVE. Alhalla; or the Lord of Talladege. A Tale of the Greek War. 12mo. pp. 118. $1 50. New York, 1843.

Henry R. Schoolcraft was the author of the poem named above. At the time of publication it would appear he adopted the name of Colcraft, *which has subsequently been abandoned for his present cognomen.*

COLDEN, CADWALLADER. An Explanation of the First Causes of Action and Matter; and of the Cause of Gravitation. 8vo. pp. 75. $10 00. *New York, printed*, 1745. *London, reprinted*, 1746.

This is without doubt an uncommonly rare book. No copy of it is known to belong to any public library in the country. It possesses considerable interest from the fact that it is an early New York production, by so celebrated a personage as the last Lieutenant-Colonel Governor of the Province. It is bound with other four tracts on a kindred subject.

COLDEN, CADWALLADER D. Memoir, Prepared at the Request of a Committee of the Common Council of the city of New York, and presented to the Mayor of the city, at the Celebration of the Completion of the New York Canals. 4to. pp. 406. Half calf, 5 portraits; 34 plates; 5 maps; 12 fac-simile letters. $10 00. New York, 1825.

COLUMBIAN MAGAZINE, THE. Or Monthly Miscellany. From the commencement, Sept., 1786 to Dec., 1792, inclusive. Complete, with the exception of the last six numbers of 1790. 7 vols. 8vo. Excessively rare. $50 00. Philadelphia, 1786, 1782.

This is the first Magazine published in America after the Revolution. It is adorned with a number of portraits, views, local maps, &c., &c. It has become very scarce; indeed, complete copies could not be procured.

CONVENTION OF DELEGATES, Minutes of the, from the Synod of New York and Philadelphia, and from the Associations of Connecticut. Held annually from 1766 to 1775, inclusive. 8vo. pp. 68. 75 cts. Hartford, 1843.

COX, DANIEL. A Description of the English Province of *Carolina*, by the Spaniards called *Florida*, and by the French *La-Louisiana*; and also of the Great and Famous River *Meschacebe* or *Missisipi*; the Five vast Navigable Lakes of Fresh Warter, and the Parts Adjacent. Together with an Account of the Commodities of the Growth and Production of the said Province, and a Preface containing some Considerations on the Consequences of the French making Settlements there. 12mo. Old calf, neat. pp. 174. With 2 maps. London, 1727.

In fine condition, $5 00.

CROTON WATER Report, various. New York, 1833-45.

CUSICK, DAVID Sketches of Ancient History of the *Six Nations*, comprising first, A Tale of the Foundation of the *Great Island* (now North America), the two Infants Born, and the creation of the Universe; Second, A Real account of the Early Settlers of North America, and their Descendants; Third, Origin of the kingdom of the Five Nations, which was called A Long House; The wars, Fierce animals, &c., with four rude wood cuts. 8vo. pp. 35. $6 00. Lockport, 1848.

What invests this pamphlet with more than ordinary interest, is the fact of its being the production of a pure blooded *North American Indian, belonging to one of the Tribes of the Five Nations, whose scanty remnants now inhabit Western New York and Canada Of course Cusick had a certain amount of education, as many of his tribe have, or he could not have produced this pamphlet, defective as it is in orthography and syntax. It has become extremely scarce; so much so that a veteran book collector informed me that he made a journey, from Albany to Lockport, a distance of over three hundred miles, and then hired a Carriage to take him twenty miles into the interior, where Cusick had spent the latter portion of his life, solely for the purpose of obtaining a copy; but his efforts proved unsuccessful; no copy could he find among the Indians or any of the whites inhabiting this region. He tried to induce an old chief to procure and send him the book some future day, by placing in his hand five dollars. He added, with evident disappointment, "I have never heard of the book, the five dollars, nor the old chief, to this day."* ....Western Memorabilia.

D'HERRERA, ANTOINE. Histoire Generale des voyages et conquestes des Castillans dans Isles & Terre-Ferme des Indes Occidentales. Par N. De La Coste. Ou l'on voit la prise de la grande ville de Mexique, &c. 4to. pp. 1818. $5. Paris, 1671.

DAGGETT, NAPHTALI. The faithful serving of God and our generation, the only Way to a peaceful and happy Death. A Sermon occasioned by the death of The Rev. Thomas Clap, (President of Yale college, in New Haven,) who departed this life Jan. 7th, 1767; Delivered in the colledge-chapel Jan. 8th. 4to. pp. 38. $3 00. New Haven, 1767.

DAVENPORT, JOHN. The Power of Congregational Churches asserted and vindicated. In answer to a Treatise of Mr. J. Paget, Intituled The Defence of Church Government, exercised in Classes and Synods. 18mo. pp. 187. $10 00. London, 1672.

E. B. Corwin's copy sold for $12.

DEBATES in the House of Delegates of Virginia, in December, 1798, on Resolutions before the House on the Acts of Congress, called the Alien and Sedition Laws. 8vo. pp. 182. Richmond, 1829. The Resolutions of Virginia and Kentucky, Penned by Madison and Jefferson, in Relation to the Alien and Sedition Laws. 8vo. pp. 76. The two bound in one. $2 50. Richmond, 1826.

DE CORDOVA, J. Observations and Laws Relating to Texas Lands, and claims against the Late Republic of Texas, by J. De Cordova, General Land Agent. 12mo. pp. 15. 75 cts. Texas, 1848.

DELAPLAINE'S Repository of the Lives and Portraits of Distinguished American Characters. 4to. 3 parts in one volume. 18 Portraits. Frontispiece. pp. 348. $6. Phil'a, 1815.

DENTON, DANIEL. A Brief History of New York, formerly New Netherlands. A new edition, with copious notes, by the Hon. Gabriel Furman. 8vo. *Fine Paper, cloth.* $1 00. New York, 1845.

DENTON, DANIEL. A Brief History of New York, formerly New Netherlands. New edition, with copious notes, by the Hon. Gabriel Furman. 4to. Fine Paper. $5. New York, 1845.

Only 100 *copies were printed upon paper of quarto size.*

"*This is the first printed description, in the English language, of the country now forming the wealthy and populous States of New York and New Jersey; but being under one government at that time* (1670). *And so great was the rarity of this book, that until the importation of the volume from which this small edition has been printed, but two copies were known to exist in the United States; one in the State Library at Albany, and the other in the Collection of Harvard University.*

A copy of the original edition was lately sold at a public sale in the city for $31 ! ! !

DEXTER, LORD TIMOTHY (*the first and only American Lord*). The Life of, embracing Sketches of the Eccentric Characters that composed his associates, by Samuel L. Knapp, including his Lordship's "*Pickles for the Knowing Ones, or Plain Truths in a Homspun Dress. Rude Portrait in full length.* 18mo. pp. 143. $2. Very rare. Newburyport, 1848.

DISH OF FROGS, THE. A Dramatic Sketch, Presented to his Royal Highness, the Prince of Imu. By Monsieur Soupetard. 18mo. pp. 28. $1. New York, 1839.

DOBBS, ARTHUR. An account of the countries adjoining to Hudson's Bay, in the north-west part of America, containing a description of their Lakes and Rivers, the Nature of the Soil and Climates, and their Methods of Commerce, &c. 4to. pp. 211. $3. London, 1744.

This Book contains a short Vocabulary of the Language spoke among the Northern Indians inhabiting the north-west part of Hudson's Bay.

DRAKE, SIR FRANCIS. Reviued calling upon the Dull or Effeminate Age, to folowe his Noble Steps for Golde & Silver, by this Memorable Relation, of the Rare occurrances (never yet declared to the World) in a third voyage made by him into the West Indies, in the Years 72 & 73. Faithfully taken out of the Reporte of Mr. Christofer Ceely, Ellis, Hixon, and others who were in the same Voyage with him. By Philip Nichols, Preacher. Reviewed also by S[r] Francis Drake himselfe, before his Death. 4to. pp. 101. 15 pp. MSS. $5 50. London, 1626.

DU TERTRE, DEAN BAPTISTE. Histoire Generale, des Isles des Christophe, de la Guadeloupe, de la Martinique, et autres dans L'Amerique. Ou l'on verra l'establissement des Colonies Francoises, dans ces Isles; leurs guerres Ciuiles & Estrangers, & tout ce quise passe dans les voyages & retours des Indes. Comme aussi plusieurs belles particularitez des Antisles de l'Amerique. Une description generale de l'Isle de la Guadeloupe; de tous ses Mineraux, de ses Pierreries, de ses Riuieres, Fontaines & Estangs; & de toutes ses Plantes. 4to. pp. 481. Map. $5 00 Paris, 1654.

EDSALL, BENJ. B., and Rev. I. F. Tuttle. The First Sussex Centennary, containing the Addresses of. With Notes, Appendix, &c. 8vo. pp. 102. $1 50. Newark, 1854.

ELLIOT, JOHN, & SAMUEL JOHNSON. A Dictionary, comprising the choisest words found in the best English Authors. 2d ed. Sm. pock't 4to. $3. Suffield, 1800.

This early attempt at compiling an Anglo-American Dictionary appears to be recommended by Theodore Dwight, Noah Webster, Benjamin Trumbull, D. D., and sixteen other notables. It is quite a curiosity in American Lexicography.

FANNY, CONTINUED. (*A Poem.*) 8vo. pp. 29. $5 00. New York, 1820.

This ingenious imitation and continuation of one of the most celebrated American poems, Fanny, was written by Isaac S. Clason, author of the XVII & XVIII Cantos of Don Juan Horace in New York, &c.

FENELON (*Archbishop of Cambry*). Dissertation on Pure Love with an account of the Life and Writings of a Lady, for whose sake the Archbishop was banished from court, and the grievous persecutions she suffered in France for her religion, also Two Letters written by one of the Lady's maids, during her confinement in the Castle of Vicennes, where she was a prisoner for eight years; one of the letters was writ with a Bit of Stick instead of a Pen, and Soot instead of Ink, to her brother; the other to a Clergyman, together with an Apologetic Preface, containing divers Letters of the Archbishop of Cambry, to the Duke of Burgundy, the present French King's Father, and other persons of distinction: also divers Letters of the Lady to Persons of Quality, relating to her Religious Principles. 12 mo. Old calf. pp. 217. $3 00. Germantown, Pa. 1750.

FIELD, DAVID D. The Genealogy of the Brainard Family, in the United States, with Sketches of Individuals. *Five Portraits.* 8vo. pp. 303. $5. N. York, 1857.

FIELDS, JAMES T. Poems. 16 mo. pp. 128. Printed on thick paper, and bound in olive morocco. Presentation copy to Rufus W. Griswold, with the author's autograph. *Privately printed.* $3 00. Cambridge, *Sine Anno.*

FINDLEY, WILLIAM. Observations on "The two Sons of Oil," containing a vindication of the American Constitutions, and defending the blessings of Religious Liberty and Toleration, against the illiberal strictures of the Rev. Samuel B. Wylie. 12 mo. pp. 366. $2. Pittsburgh, 1812.

FOX, GEORGE. Memoirs of the Life of, By Henry Tuke. 12mo. pp. 327. $1 00. Philadelphia, 1815.

It is not generally known that the venerable George Fox was quite a voluminous writer. But so he was. The list of his published Treatises amounts to no less than 115; *all of which are enumerated at the end of Tuke's Life of him.*

FRANKLIN, BENJAMIN, The Works of. 6 vols. 8vo. Boards. $6 75. Philadelphia, 1819.

FRANKLIN, BENJAMIN. Rules for Reducing a Great Empire to a small one. To which is subjoined the Declaration of Independence. 8vo. pp. 16. $1 00. London, 1703.

FRANKLIN, BENJAMIN. M. T. Cicero's Cato Major, or discourse on Old Age. Addressed to Titus Pomponius Atticus, With explanatory notes. By Benj. Franklin, LL. D. 8vo. Boards. $3 00. London, 1778.

FRIENDLY ADDRESS, The. To all Reasonably Americans, on the Subject of our Political Confusions; carefully abridged from the original. 8vo. pp. 24. $2 00. New York, 1774.

FRIBBLETON, GEORGE. Ex-Barber to his Majesty the king of Great Britain. Travels in America. 12mo. pp. 216. $1 50. New York, 1833.

This is one among the very many spirited and clever imitations of the renowned Baron Munchausen's Travels. The object of the author was to hold up to ridicule the many European Tourists who have, from time to time, visited America and published the results of their experiences, observations, and disappointments, frequently rather wide of the truth. The Author's name was Asa Greene, M. D. who had been brought up in New England to the Medical profession, but not succeeding in the calling removed to New York about 1830. *Here he commenced Editor, Author and Bookseller. For some time he conducted a popular penny paper entitled the Transcript. He was author of several books, among them, the best known is the Adventures of Dodimus Duckworth, the quack Steam Doctor. Perhaps no American author of his time surpassed him in quaint, genuine humor. The last named book exhibits exquisite specimens of these traits, as well as his travels of the Ex-Barber. He was found dead in his bookstore, corner of Theatre Alley and Beekman street, about* 1839. *His death much surprised his friends as none of them ever knew that he had been ailing. In physiognomy he bore a strong resemblance to the celebrated Aaron Burr, small black, twinkling eye, dark, leathery, dead complexion, and a solemn, sedate aspect, seldom looking mirthful or even pleased.*

....Western Memorabilia.

GAGE, THOMAS. The English-American, his travail by Sea and Land; or, A New Survey of the West Indies, containing A Journall of Three thousand and Three hundred Miles within the main land of America. Wherein is set forth his Voyage from Spain to St. de John Vlhua; and from thence to Xalappa, to Tlaxcalla, the City of Angeles, and forward to Mexico; With the description of that great city as it was in former times, and also at this present. Likewise his Journey from Mexico through the Provinces of Guaxaca, Chiapa, Gautemala, Vera Paz, Truxillo, Comayagua; with his abode Twelve years Gautemala, and especially in the Indian-towns of Mixco; Pinóla, Petapa, Amatitlam. Folio. pp. 236. $6 00. London, 1648.

GALLAHER, JAMES. The Western Sketch Book. 12mo. 408. $1.25. Boston, 1850.

GALLATIN, ALBERT. A Sketch of the Finance of the United States. 8vo. pp. 202. $2 00. New York, 1796.

GARRARD, LEWIS H. Chambersburg in the Colony and the Revolution. A Sketch. 8vo. pp. 60. $1 50. Philadelphia, 1856.

GLENN, JAMES. The Cap Against the Cowl. The Lecture Room and Laboratory Versus the Pulpit and the Cloister. 4to. pp. 129. MS. New York, 1855.

GOVERNMENT OF THE UNITED STATES. An Exposition of the Weakness and Inefficiency of. 12mo. pp. 380. $5 00 *Unique Stained.* Privately Printed. *Sine Loco,* 1845.

No sooner did this book make its appearance but it was immediately called in or suppressed on account of its libelous character against all free governments, but more especially that of the United States. The author's name is unknown, but it is supposed he was at one time in high office in the American Government.

GRAINGER, JAMES. The Sugar Cane: a poem in four books. With notes and frontispiece. pp. 167. London, 1764. To which is added, The ancient English Wake: Poem by Mr. Jerningham. pp. 21. London, 1779. Also, Poems by a young Nobleman, of Distinguished Abilities, lately deceased; Particularly the State of England, and the once flourishing City of London, In a letter from an American Traveller, Dated from the

Ruinous Portico of St. Paul's, in the Year 2199, To a friend settled in Boston, the Metropolis of the Western Empire. Also, Sundry Fugitive Pieces, principally wrote whilst upon his Travels on the continent. pp. 60. London, 1780. In one vol. 4to. $5 00.

GRAY, JAMES. The fiend of the Reformation detected. Part 1, the two sophisms detected, which have split the reformers into calvinist, arminians, Redemptional universalist, &c. Part 2, a brief Review of the Present State of the Reformed churches; their controversies, sermons, theological seminaries, some of the chief causes of their divisions assigned, and some hints suggested Respecting the cure of their schisms. 8vo. pp. 144. $1 00. Philadelphia, 1817.

GREBO LANGUAGE. A brief Grammatical Analysis of the Grebo Language. 8vo. pp. 36. 1 50. Cape Palmas, Africa, 1838.

GREENHOW, ROBERT. Memoir, Historical and Political, on the Northwest Coast of North America, and the adjacent Territories; illustrated by a map and a Geographical view of those countries. 8vo. pr. pp. 228. $1 00. Paper. Washington, 1840

GRIFFITHS, JOHN. A collection of the Newest Cotillions, and Country Dances; principally composed by J. G., Dancing Master; to which is added, instances of ill-manners, to be carefully avoided by youth of both Sexes. Small 4to. pp. 15. $5 00. Troy, N. Y., 1795.

This is the first treatise on dancing that has been printed and published in the United States. It is quite a shabby pamphlet both as to typography and paper. It proves two things, namely: that printing was carried on at this early day in the then village of Troy, probably then numbering but a few hundreds of inhabitants, now numbering 36,000; and that dancing must have then been a popular amusement, for the village contained not only a teacher of that art, but produced a treatise on the subject, which it may be safely asserted that no other city, town or village in the United States had done.

HALCYON ITINERARY, THE; and the Millenium Messenger. 18mo. pp. 224. $5 00. Marietta, Ohio, 1807.

This must be one of the first books of a miscellaneous character printed in the State of Ohio.

HALCYON LUMINARY, THE, and Theological Repository, a monthly Magazine, devoted to Religion and Polite Literature; conducted By a Society of Gentlemen. In 2 vols. 8vo. pp 590–575. $3 00. New York, 1812.

This periodical was, in its day, the organ of New Jerusalem church denomination in America. It abounds with able and interesting articles. The American poet, Woodworth, author of the "Old oaken bucket," was, I believe, at one time co-editor of the work. It ended with the termination of the second volume; a longer life than more than two-thirds of the American magazines enjoy.

HAMILTON, ALEXANDER. The Works of. Comprising his correspondence, and his political and official writings, exclusive of the Federalist, civil and military, published from the original manuscripts, deposited in the Department of State. Edited by John C. Hamilton. 7 vols. 8vo. cloth. $55 00. New York, 1851.

HANCOCK, JOHN, Ten Chapters in the Life of. Originally published under the name of the Writings of Saco, in 1789. 8 vo. pp. 68. Cloth, $3 00. (*Privately printed.*) New York, 1857.

HARLAN, RICHARD. Fauna Americana; being a description of the *Mammiferous Animals* inhabiting North America. 8vo. pp. 317. $2 00. Philadelphia, 1825.

HASSLER, FERD. ROD. Comparison of Weights and Measures, of Length and Capacity, reported to the Senate of the United States by the Treasury Department in 1832. 8vo. Half calf. pp. 122. Plates $2 00. Washington, 1832.

HAWKINS, THOMAS. The Book of the Great Sea-Dragons, Ichthyosauri and Plesiosauri, Gedolim Taninim, of Moses, extinct monsters of the ancient earth, with Thirty large Plates, copied from skeletons in the Author's collection of Fossil Organic Remains. (Deposited in the British Museum.) Large folio. $3 00. London, 1840.

HICKS, ELIAS. Journal of the Life and Religious Labors. Written by himself. 8vo. *Fine portrait.* $2 25. N. York, 1832.

HICKS, ELIAS. Two Sermons delivered in New York, 1st mo. 31st, 1830. 8vo. pp. 32. 63 cts. New York, 1831.

HICKS, ELIAS, The Last Letter of. Written Hugh Judge, of Ohio. 8vo. pp. 6. 50 cts. Jericho, 1830.

Friend Elias was the Peter the Hermit, the Luther, the Knox and the Wesley among the broad-brims and drab coats, during his pilgrimage. Like all innovators or reformers he was held up by the party who adopted his views and sentiments as a genuine reformer, as having opened the eyes of the blind, and as an apostle little less than St. Paul, while on the other hand, those opposed to him denounced him as a disturber of the peace, a pestilent fellow, and a coadjutor of the devil........ Western Memorabilia.

HICKCOX, JOHN H. An Historical Account of American Coinage. Plates. Royal 8vo. pp. 147. $5 00. Albany, 1858.

HOOKER, THOS. A survey of the summe of Church Discipline. Wherein the Way of the Churches of New England is warranted out of the Word, and all exceptions of weight, which are made against it, answered. Whereby also it will appear to the Judicious Reader that something more must be said, than yet hath been, before their principles can be shaken, or they should be unsettled in their practice. 4to. pp. 479. $5 00. London, 1648.

HOSMER, H. L. Early History of the Maumee Valley. 8vo. pp. 70. $1 00. Toledo, 1858.

IRVING, WASHINGTON. A History of New York, from the beginning of the World to the end of the Dutch Dynasty, containing among many surprising and curious matters, the unutterable ponderings of Walter the Doubter, the Disastrous Projects of William the Testy, and the Chivalric Achievements of Peter the Headstrong, the three Dutch Governors of New Amsterdam, being the only authentic history of the times that ever hath been published. 2 vols. 12mo. pp. 292 and 248. Portrait and a view of New York in 1640. $5 00. Phila. 1812.

This is the second edition of this remarkable book. It is adorned with a full length portrait of DEDERICK KNICKERBOCKER, *the fictitious historian, and a view of New Amsterdam (now New York) as it appeared about the year* 1640.

INDIAN SPEECHE AN. In Answer to a sermon preached by a Sweedish Missionary at Conastogo, in Pennsylvania. To which is added a brief account of the Vision and death of the late Lord Littleton, also Lord Kames' Anecdote of the melancholy end of a Profligato Young Man. 12mo. pp. 12. $1. Stanford, 1806.

JOHN BULL. The diverting history of John Bull and Brother Jonathan. *By Hector Bull-us.* 18mo. pp. 135. $5 00. Rough Calf,—very fine preservation. New York, 1812.

KENNET, BASIL. Twenty Sermons preached on several occasions, to a Society of British Merchants in Foreign Parts. 8vo. Calf. pp. 358. $1 50. London, 1727.

KEY, FRANCIS S. Poems of the late, author of the "Star Spangled Banner," with an Introductory Letter by Chief Justice Taney. 12mo. Mor. full gilt. very neat. A splendid copy. pp. 203. $3 00. New York, 1857.

LATER FROM HELL, or, Philotheologiastronomos' eulogism of Rev. Ezra Stiles Ely's Dream. 8vo. pp. 30. 75 cts. Philadelphia, 1825.

LEDYARD, JOHN. A Journal of Captain Cook's last Voyage to the Pacific Ocean, and in quest of a North-west Passage, between Asia and America; performed in the years 1776, 1777, 1778 and 1779. 8vo pp. 208. $3 00. Hartford, 1783.

LE GENTIL. Nouveau voyage au tour du monde. Enrichi de Plusieurs Plans, Vûes and Perspectives des Principles villes and Ports du Pérou, Chily, Bresil, et de la Chine avec une description de l'Empire de la Chine, beaucoup plus ample et plus circonstanciée que celles qui ont paru jusqu'a Present, oû il est traiti des Mœurs, Religion, Politique, Education et Commerce, des Peuples de cet Empire. 12mo. 3 vols. in 1. Plates and Maps. $2 50. Amsterdam, 1728.

LETTER from the Secretary of State to Charles C. Pinckney, Esq., in answer to the complaints of the French Minister against the Government of the United States, contained in his notes to the Secretary of State, dated the 27th of October, and the 15th of November, 1796. 12mo. pr. pp. 54. $1 00. New York, 1797.

LIGON, RICHARD, Gent. A true and exact history of the Island of Barbados. Illustrated with a map of the Island, as also the principal trees and plants there, set forth in their due proportions and shapes, drawne out by their severall and respective scale. Together with the Ingenio that makes the Sugar, with the Plots of the severall Houses, Roomes, and other places, that are used in the whole process of Sugar making; viz: the Grinding-room, the Boyling-room, the Filling room, the Curing House, Still House, and Furnace. All cut in Copper. Folio. pp. 124. $6 00. London, 1657.

LOCKE, JOHN. A Collection of Several Pieces of; never before printed, or not extant in his works. 8vo. pp. 441. $1 50. London, 1720.

This volume contains the fundamental Constitution of Carolina by Mr. Locke, besides many curious pieces.

LOCKE, RICHARD ADAMS. The Moon Hoax, or the discovery that the Moon has a vast population of Human Beings. Illustrated with a view of the Moon as seen by Lord Ross' Telescope. 8vo. pp. 63. 50 cts. New York, 1859.

LOCO-FOCOISM, as displayed in the Boston Magazine against Schools and Ministers, and in favor of robbing children of the property of their parents! Christians! Patriots! Fathers! read and reflect! 8vo. pp. 32. $1 00. Albany, 1840.

MACLAURIAN LYCEUM, Contributions to Arts and Sciences. 3 parts all published. *Plates.* $2 00. Philadelphia, 1827–29.

MAPS. (In Miniature on one Sheet.) With the depth of water of the Harbours of the principal English, French and Spanish Towns in America. Among them New York, Boston, Louisbourg, Charles-town, Havana, Quenca, Martinico, &c. 14 by 18 inches. $5 00. London, 1739.

MARSH, GEORGE P. The Goths in New England. A Discourse delivered at the Anniversary of the Philomathesian Society of Middlebury College. Aug. 15, 1848. 8vo. pp. 39. $1 25. Middlebury, 1843.

MARVIN, HENRY. A Complete History of Lake George, embracing a great variety of information and compiled with an especial reference to meet the wants of the travelling community, intended as a descriptive guide together with a complete history and present appearance of Ticonderoga. 18mo. pp. 102. Map. $1 50. New York, 1853.

MATHEMATICAL CORRESPONDENT, The, Containing new elucidations, discoveries and improvements in various branches of mathematics. *With a fine head of George Baron*, engraved by Dr. Anderson, Vol. I. 12mo. pp. 248. *Very rare.* $2 00. New York, 1804.

MATTER. The Elements of, discovered and Explained; in which the Nature of Space, the Combination of the Elements in the formation of matter; the Origin of celestial bodies; The principles of Gravitation, Locomotion, &c., &., are exhibited in such Plain and Simple views, with References to the Phenomena as they exist in nature, that they cannot be mistaken. Plates. 8vo. pp. 45. $1 00. New York, 1836.

McALPINE, J. Genuine Narratives, and concise Memoirs of some of the most Interesting Exploits and Singular Adventures of I. McAlpine, a native Highlander, from the time of his Emigration from Scotland to America, 1773; during the Long period of his faithful attachment to, and hazardous attendance on British Armys, under the command of the Generals Carelton and Burgoyne, in their several operations that He was concerned in; till December, 1779. To complain of his Neglected services; and Humbly to Request Government for Reparation of his Losses in the Royal cause. Every circumstance Related Faithfully, and with all delicacy, containing nothing but Indisputable facts that can be well vouched, and are mostly known to many Gentlemen of good character, in both the Private and Military lines of Life; carefully arranged, and published for the use of the Publick at Large. 12mo. pp. 63. *A very rare pamphlet.* $10 00. Greenock, 1780.

McKENNEY, THOMAS L., & J. HALL. Indian Tribes of North America and their History, with Biographical Sketches and Anecdotes of the principal Chiefs. By McKenney and Hall. *With 120 large and beautifully colored portraits of the Chiefs*, from the Indian Gallery in the Department of War at Washington. Complete in 3 vols. Imperial folio. Handsomely half bound, morocco, gilt back and gilt edges. New. Pub. at $120 00 in parts. $100 00. Philadelphia, 1838.

Some years ago Col. McKenney obtained from Government permission to take copies of the Indian portraits deposited in the War Department, with a view to publication in lithograph. The design was accomplished on a large scale, and the olio edition is valued, both in Europe and America, as one of the most interesting and magnificent properties of a rich man's library. The biographies, written by Col. McKenney and James Hall, Esq., of Cincinnati, are sufficiently copious and drawn from the most authentic sources. One of those in the first number is that of Sequoyah, or George Guess, the inventor of the Cherokee alphabet; a remarkable man, having in his character and appearance much more of the Oriental than of the American red man. Another portrait of great interest is that of an Osage woman; a face remarkable for beauty and intelligent expression.

MEMORIALS. Written on several occasions during the Illness and after the Decease of *Three Little* Boys. A collection of Mournful Poems Supposed to have been written by W. H. Parmly. 8vo. pp. 52. $1 00. New York, 1842.

MILITARY DISCIPLINE. A New System of, founded upon principle, By a General Officer. 8vo. pp. 258. $1 50. Philadelphia, 1776.

MILITARY JOURNALS, THE, of two Private Soldiers, 1758—1775, with numerous Illustrative Notes, to which is added a Supplement containing official Papers on the Skirmishes at Lexington and Concord. 8vo. pp. 128. $2. Poughkeepsie, 1855.

MILLER, STEPHEN F. The Bench and Bar of Georgia; Memoirs and Sketches. With an Appendix, containing a Court Roll from 1790 to 1857. 2 vols. 8vo. pp. 937. $4 00. Philadelphia, 1858.

MINNESOTA. Annals of the Minnesota Historical Society. Materials for the future History of Minnesota; being a Report of the Minnesota Historical Society to the Legislative Assembly. To which is added an Address delivered before the Historical Society at its sixth anniversary, Feb. 1st, 1856, by the Hon. H. H. Sibley. *Five wood cuts and Portrait of Jonathan Carver.* Royal 8vo. pp. 149.. $1 50. St. Pauls, Min., 1856.

MINSHULL, JOHN (*the American Cibber*). Rural Felicity: a Comic Opera; with the Humor of Patrick and Marriage of Shelty. 8vo. pp. 69. Portrait by Scoles. $3 50. New York, 1801.

MINSHULL, JOHN. The Sprightly Widow with the Frolics of Youth; or, a Speedy Way to Unite the Sexes by Honorable Marriage. pp. 64. 1802. She Stoops to Conquer; or, the Virgin Wife Triumphant: a Comedy in three Acts. pp. 30. 1804 Mary's Dream; Humorous Triumph over the Poet in Petticoats, and the Gallant Exploits of the Knight of the Comb: a Comedy in three Acts. pp. 29. All bound in one. $6 00. Fine Portrait by Scoles. New York, 1804.

Minshull was a prominent New York citizen about the end of the last century. He was the author of several plays, which do not possess very much merit and are now entirely forgotten, and indeed could not perhaps be procured.

........................Western Memorabilia.

MIRROR, THE NEW. Of Literature, Amusement, and Instruction, containing Tales of Romance, Sketches of Society, Manners and every day Life, Domestic and Foreign Correspondence, Wit and Humour, Fashion and Gossip, the Fine Arts and Literary, Musical and Dramatic Criticism. Extracts from New Works, Poetry, Original and Select, the Spirit of Public Journals, &c., &c. *Numerous fine Plates.* 3 vols. royal 8vo. Half bound in morocco. $6 50.
New York, 1843–1844.

MOORE, FRANCIS. A Voyage to Georgia, begun in the year 1735. Containing an account of the settling the town of Frederica, in the southern part of the province, and a description of the Soil, Air, Birds, Beasts, Trees, Rivers, Islands, &c., with the rules and orders made by the Honorable the trustees for that settlement; including the allowances of Provisions, Clothing, and other necessaries to the Families and servants which went thither. Also a description of the town and county of Savannah, in the northern part of the province; the manner of dividing and granting the lands and the improvement there, with an account of the Air, Soil, Rivers and Islands in that part. 8vo. pp. 108. $5.
London, 1744.

MORGAN, JOHN (M. D.). A discourse upon the Institution of Medical Schools in America; delivered at a public Anniversary Commencement, held in the College of Philadelphia, May 30, and 31, 1765. 8vo. pp. 91. $10 00.
Philadelphia, 1765.

This book is a great curiosity, both in respect to typography as well as Medical history. It is undoubtedly among the first of American medical productions, and what renders it still more valuable, it is from the press of the son of the American Caxton, William Bradford. This copy is in good preservation and in the original binding. Corwin's copy, although much inferior, sold for $9 50.

MORSE, JEDIDIAH. A Report to the Secretary of War of the United States, of Indian Affairs, comprising a Narrative of a tour performed in the summer of 1820, under a commission from the President of the United States, for the purpose of ascertaining, for the use of the Government, the actual state of the Indian tribes in our country. Illustrated by a map of the United States; ornamented by a correct portrait of a Pawnee Indian. 8vo. pp. 400. $2 00. Very fine copy. Uncut. New Haven, 1822.

MORTON, SAMUEL GEORGE. Crania Americana; or a Comparative view of the *Skulls of various Aboriginal Nations of North and South America.* To which is prefixed an Essay on the Varieties of the Human Species. Illustrated by seventy-eight plates and a colored map. Folio. pp. 297. $33 00. *Very scarce.*
Philadelphia, 1829.

NARRATIVE OF AN EXPEDITION to the east coast of Greenland, sent by order of the king of Denmark, in search of the Lost Colonies, under the command of Capt. W. A. Graah, of the Danish Royal Navy, Knight of Dannebrog, &c Translated from the Danish, By the Late G. Gordon Macdougall, F. R. S. N. A., With the Original Danish chart completed by the Expedition. 8vo. pp. 216. $2.
London, 1837.

NATIONAL PORTRAITS, Catalogue of, in Independent Hall, Philadelphia, comprising many of the signers of the Declaration of Independence, and many others. 8vo. pp. 23. 50 cts. Phila., 1858.

NEWARK (NEW JERSEY). Directory of the city of, for 1855–56. Map of the city. 12mo. pp. 432. Compiled by *B. T. Pierson.* $1. Newark, N. J., 1855.

NEW YORK COLONIAL HISTORY. Documents relative to the Colonial History of the State of New York; procured in Holland, England and France, by John Romeyn Brodhead, Esq., Agent. Edited E. B. O'Callaghan, M. D., LL. D. With a general Introduction by the agent. 11 vols. 4to. Clo. Maps, &c. $30 00.
Albany, 1856–60.

NEW YORK DIRECTORIES. From 1804 to 1860, inclusive, with the exception of 1805–8–9. 55 vols. 12mo. and 8vo. $300 00. New York, 1804–60.

There can be no better chronological step-ladder for presenting in a clear light the gradual growth or decline of a city than a consecutive series of its directories, giving annually the number of houses, with the names of the respective householders thereof, public institutions and private enterprises, &c. Here are facts without fiction or coloring; a solid base for correct estimate; in short, a reliable reference book not to be doubted. It must be remembered that statistics is the corner stone of history; without them history would degenerate into romance and unmeaning fiction. A series of New York Directories form a perfect miniature of the rise and progress of the American Metropolis.

NEW YORK. Document of the Board of Aldermen. Report on laying out the new park. With a colored map of the same. 8vo. Paper. $1 00.
New York, 1852.

NEW YORK State Library Catalogue. In Four Departments, namely: General Literature, Law, Maps, and Bibliography. 4 vols. Royal 8vo. ½ morocco. $10.
Albany, 1856.

NEW YORK. The Natural History of the State of New York, with an astonishing profusion of Plates—some colored; and a lengthy Introduction by the Hon. William H. Seward. 19 vols. 4to. Map. $110 00. Albany, 1842–55.

NIAGARA FALLS. Table Rock Album, or Sketches of the Falls and Scenery Adjected. 12mo. pp. 108. $1 25. Buffalo, 1850.

Among the contributers to this Album will be found the names of Lords Morpeth and Durham, Sir Francis Head, Rev. J. Dowling, John G. Saxe, Willis Gaylord Clark, J. S. Buckingham, and over one hundred others.

NEW YORK CITY. Corporation Manuals. From the commencement in 1841 to 1860. With numerous Fac-similies, Maps, View and Plates. 18 vols. 24mo., 18mo., and 12mo. *Compiled by David Valentine.* $30 New York, 1841–60.

This series of books (The New York Corporation Manuals) has become an important item in the Antiquarian, Historical, Biographical and Literary annals of the city of New York. To those desiring information about the city, or who may be writing on the subject, will find these books indispensible repositories of information. Mr. Valentine deserves well, and more than well, of the community, and of posterity which will come after him, for having been such a faithful and judicious gleaner of these scattered historic fragments and antiquarian facts, and giving them a shape which will command respect, as well as to secure them a permanency. The eollection of facsimiles and maps alone, say nothing of the engraved views, are of great intrinsic value, and possess a charming interest to all who love to contemplate past transactions.

.... Western Memorabilia.

NOURSE, JAMES. The New Testament of our Lord and Saviour, Jesus Christ; Translated out of the Original Greek, and with the former Translations diligently compared and revised. The Text of the common Translation is arranged in paragraphs, such as the sense requires; the division of chapters and verses being noted in the margin, for reference. By *James Nourse, A. M.* 8vo. pp. About $2 00. Philadelphia, 1829.

OLDMIXON, JOHN. The British Empire in America, containing the History of the Discovery, Settlement, Progress and State of the British Colonies on the Continent and Islands of America. 2 vols. 8vo. Calf. pp. 601 and 478. Maps. Fine copy. $5 00. London, 1741.

OTIS, JAMES. The Rights of the British Colonies asserted and proved. Third Edition, corrected. 8vo. pp. 120. $2 50. Boston, N. E., 1766.

OTT, JAMES CRAMER. The Truth according to and with the World. $1 50. Albany, 1850.

OXFORD ACADEMY JUBILEE, Held at Oxford, Chenango County, N. Y., August 1st and 2d, 1854. *Four fine steel portraits*; viz: Henry W. Rogers, R. W. Juliand, John Tracy and Horatio Seymour. 8vo. pp. 130. $2 00. New York, 1856.

PAINE, THOMAS. An Extraordinary Collection of Pamphlets by, for and against this celebrated man. Among them his Trial for Blasphemy and the Trial of his book seller for publishing and selling his pamphlets, &c., &c. In all, 40. $10. London, V. D.

PAMPHLETS. An extraordinary collection of pamphlets, chiefly American, consisting of Speeches, Orations, Addresses, Lectures, Biography, Local History, Sermons, Political Discussions, Banking, Poetry, and on a great variety of other subjects. Bound up in 310 vols. 8vo. $930. V. D.

A manuscript catalogue, giving the full title, number of pages, where published, and date, will accompany the collection. This formidable body of pamphlets cost the collector fifteen years' labor in bringing them together.

Pamphlets having this considerable advantage, that, springing from some immediate occasion they are copied more directly from the life; so likelier to bear a resemblance than any more extended draughts taken by a remote light; the writers have a less opportunity to comment, and their writings are less liable to admit such foul and frequent practices of plagiary as books of matter more various, and bulk more voluminous, too often exhibit. Besides, the author being more vigorously prompted to application by the expediency to bring forth his work, opportunity is urged to shake out the image of his mind at a heat, in the most natural form and symmetry, in the most significant circumstances at once, seldom allowing leisure for the writer to dote upon or dream over his work, whether to disguise it with the conceptions of other men nor to deform it with chimeras of his own. Hence they are preferred by many critics to discover the genuine abilities of the author and the true map of the time or things before the more dilatory and accumulated productions.

..........F. Morgan's Phœnix Britannicus.

PANCIROLLI GUIDONIS. Rerum Memorabilium sive deperditarum Pars Prior commentarijs illustrata et focis prope innumeris postremum aucta ab Henrico Salmuth Ambergensium Sijndico Emerito. 4to. pp. 372, also, Clarissimi Nova Reperta sive Rerum Memoribilium Recens Inventarum and verteribus incognitorum Pars Posterion; Ex Italico latini reddita nec non commentariis illustrata et locis prope innumeris postremum aucta ab Henrico Salmuth Ambergensium syndico emerito. 4to. pp. 328. $4 00. Francofurti, 1631.

PATENT OFFICE REPORT for 1843. pp. 335. 8vo. uncut and unbound, $3 00. *very rare.* Washington, D. C.

PATENT RIGHT OPPRESSION Exposed, or Knavery Detected in an address to unite all good people to obtain a Repeal of the Patent Laws. *A Poem with copious notes. Patrick N. J. Elisha, Esq.*, Poet Laureate, 12mo. pp. 189. *Very rare.* $1 50. Philadelphia, 1814.

PAYNE, JOHN HOWARD. Lispings of the Muses, a Selection from Juvenile Poems, chiefly written at and before the age of *sixteen*. 8vo. pp. 30. $2 00. London, 1815.

The following endorsement in the hand writing of the author is to be found upon the fly leaf:

"Isaac S. Clason, Esq., from his friend, John Howard Payne. London, Sept. 2, 1820."

Clason was by profession an actor and had acquired some celebrity both in England and America as such, but he is, or will perhaps be hereafter better known as the author of the continuation of the Don Juan cantos, XVII and XVIII, a very clever imitation of Lord Byron's style of writing; also Fanny continued, a no less remarkable imitation of the style of Fitz Greene Halleck. He died miserably in London, report says on the one hand, by starvation, on the other, by suicide. Payne died at Aleppo in 1852, while in the capacity of American consul at that place.

PENN, WILLIAM An Address to Protestants upon the present Conjuncture. In II Parts. 4to. pp. 148. $3. 1679.

PENN, WILLIAM. (Founder of Pennsylvania.) The Works of. Very neat. Calf backs and corners. Both titles lost, otherwise a desirable copy. 2 vols. folio. $6 50.

PENNSYLVANIA MAGAZINE, The, Or American Monthly Magazine (said to have been edited by Tom. Paine). 8vo. Vol. 1. pp. 490. Plates and Local Maps. *Autograph of James Abercrombie.* $10 00. *very rare.* Philadelphia, 1775.

PILPAY. The Instructive and entertaining Fables of, an ancient Indian Philosopher, containing a number of excellent *Rules* for the conduct of persons of all ages, and in all stations, under several heads. 4th Edition corrected, improved and enlarged. 8vo. pp. 127. *uncut.* $5 00. London printed, America re-printed, 1784.

Wonderfull to relate, this renowned piece of curious Antiquitie should have been printed in the United States at this early day. The book even then must have been a great rarity in Europe. and, of course, at the time almost unknown in America except among the case-hardened book-collectors, which, no doubt then a few were scattered up and down throughout the country at the time. Whoever re-printed or caused this book to be re-printed at that time must have been a great enthusiast for none else would have done it. It has affixed neither printer's name nor place where printed, but simply thus, "London printed, America Reprinted, MDCCLXXXIV."

POLITICAL REGISTER, (The) and Impartial Review of New Books. 11 vols. in 6. 8vo. treed calf. Plates in each volume. Very neat. $20 00. Published by J. Almon. London, 1767–72.

In these volumes will be found the germ of the discontent which afterwards led to the overthrow of British power in their thirteen provinces in North America by the afterwards memorable revolution. Many of the papers are of a decided RED REPUBLICAN *stamp communicated by Americans who appeared to have entertained a very unfriendly opinion of the mother country. The volumes are adorned with a number of political caricature plates; they may be said to be the harbinger to the celebrated periodical entitled,* ALMON'S AMERICAN REMEMBRANCER; *indeed, the one appears to be the necessary pendant to the other.*

PROTESTANT Episcopal Historical Society Collections. Vol. II. Containing the Life of the pioneer Missionary, Rev. Jacob Bailey. By W. S. Bartlett, with notes by Bishop Burgess. 3 portraits, 8vo. pp. 365. $2 50. New York, 1853.

PSALTERIUM AMERICANUM. The Book of Psalms, in a translation exactly conformed unto the Original, but all in blank verse, fitted unto the tunes commonly used in our churches. Which Pure Offering is accompanied with Illustrations, digging for hidden treasures in it; and Rules to employ it upon the Glorious and Various Intentions of it. Whereto are added some other portions of the Sacred Scripture, to Enrich the Cautional. 12mo. pp. 452. $40 00. Boston, in N. E., 1718.

With the exception of the "Bay Psalm Book," the first book printed in North America, this is the scarcest of all the early printed Hymn Books produced by the American press in Colonial times. This copy is in the original binding in perfect condition and apparently has never been used. The version is said to have been the production of the renowned Cotton Mather, the most voluminous writer America has produced. His publications amount in number to not less than 382. Of course many of these are single sermons and pamphlets but still there are many of them single volumes, and some of them in more than one. For a further account of this book see Hood's History of Music in New England, a book, by the by, which contains a good deal bibliographical information.

RAGUET, CONDY. The Banner of the Constitution. Devoted to General Politics, Political Economy, State Papers Foreign and Domestic. 3 vol. large folio. $10 50. Washington, 1830–32.

RAYMOND, WILLIAM. Biographical Sketches of the distinguished men of Columbia County, including an account of the most important offices they have filled. 8vo. pp. 119. $1 00. *In all 29 Biographies.* Albany, 1851.

REESE, DAVID M. Humbugs of New York: being a remonstance against Popular Delusion, whether in Science, Philosophy or Religion. 12mo. pp. 273. $1 00. New York, 1838.

REES, JAMES. The Dramatic authors of America. 12mo. pp. 144. $1 00. Philadelphia, 1845.

A work showing a considerable amount of bibliographical industry. Here is a little book giving a catalogue of one hundred and eleven American dramatic authors, with a list of their respective plays, occasional short biographical sketches, notices of some of the American Theatres throughout the country and a meagre chronology of the American Theatre.

Although the author has aimed at alphabetical arrangement his book is quite defective in this respect, as well as in others, having neither chapters, headings, prominent catch-words, chronological arrangement, contents nor index; besides he has quite defaced his book by occasionally introducing parts of scenes of certain plays which has much incumbered his performance, without adding interest or value to it. Notwithstanding all this the author deserves great credit for this performance, inasmuch as it is the first and only one of the kind (so far as I can learn) that has appeared in the country. It will be an excellent nucleus for a more extended and better arranged treatise on the same subject......... .... Western Memorabilia.

RELATIONS DES JESUITS, contenant ce qui s'est passé de plus remarquable dans les missions des Pères de la Compagnie de Jésus dans la Nouvelle France. Ouvrage publié sous les auspices du gouvernement Canadien. 3 vols. royal 8vo. of about 900 pp. each. $15 00. Paper covers. Quebec, 1858.

"This work, of which only a small number were printed, is a complete reprint of all the Jesuit Relations concerning the missions in Canada and French North America, from 1611 *to* 1672; *and contains most important matter concerning the Indian Tribes, and the early history of Maine, New York and all the Northwest."*

REJECTED ADDRESSES, The. Together with the Prize Addresses presented to the Prize Medal offered for the best Address on the opening of the New Park Theatre in the City of New York. 18mo. pp. 132. $2 00. Very rare. New York, 1821.

The following are among the contributors to this volume of fugitive pieces, namely; C. Sprague, S. Woodworth, Moses Y. Scott, James B. Sheys, Joseph Cross, M'Donald Clarke, besides about sixty anonymous contributors.

RIGGS, S. R. Grammar and Dictionary of the Dakota Language, collected by the members of the Dakota Mission. 4to. pp. 333. $6 00. Washington City, 1852.

ROBINSON, JOHN. Essayes; or, Observations, Divine and Morall. Collected out of Holy Scriptures, Ancient and Moderne Writers, both Divine and Humane. As also, out of the great volume of men's manners: Tending to the furtherance of knowledge and vertue. 2d edition with two Tables, the one of the authors quoted, the other of the matters contained in the observations. 18mo. calf, pp. 598. $10 00. London, 1638

The descendants of the pilgrims have not ceased to this day to revere the memory of John Robinson.

ROYALL, MRS. ANNE. The Black Book, or a Continuation of Travels in the United States. 3 vols. 12mo. pp. 328, 396 and 235. $6 00. Washington, 1828.

ROYALL, MRS. ANNE. Pennsylvania, or Travels Continued in the United States. 2 vols. 12mo. pp. 276 and 317. $3 00. Washington, 1829.

ROYALL, MRS. ANNE. Sketches of History, Life and Manners in the United States. By a Traveller. 12mo. pp. 392. $1 50. New York, 1826.

ROYALL, MRS. ANNE. Southern Tour, or Second Series of the Black Book. 3 vol. 8vo. pp. 181, 217, and 246. $4 00. Washington, 1831.

ROYALL, MRS. ANNE. Letters from Alabama, on various subjects; to which are added an Appendix, containing remarks on sundry Members of the 20th Congress, and other high characters at the Seat of Government. 8vo. pp. 238. $2 00. Washington, 1830.

*This Amazon would have been more appropriately employed as a fishmonger in Billingsgate Market, or a Meg Merrilies heading a gang of Gypsie Smugglers, than the author of books or editing a newspaper. She was the terror of every member of Congress while she resided at Washington, and in order to propitiate her favor, they one and all promptly subscribed for her journal "*Paul Pry."

RUSSELL, R. W. Remarks on the English Enlistment Question, with an abstract of the correspondence thereon. 8vo, pp. 103. $1 00. New York, 1856.

SAINT ANDREW'S SOCIETY, Historical Sketch of the, of the State of New York, with the constitution and list of officers and members since 1756. Centennial oration before the Society, on the 1st December, 1856, by the Rev. John Thompson, D. D. 12mo. pp. 120. $1 50. New York, 1856.

SANDYS, GEORGE. Ovid's Metamorposis. Englished by G. S. Small folio—engraved title. $5 00. London, 1662.

This is, perhaps the first attempt at writing English poetry in the New World; at all events it is without doubt the first translation of a classic author into the English tongue. Sandys was colonial secretary for the Virginia Plantations during the time he made this translation of Ovid. In his dedication to Charles 1st, he speaks thus of his performance. "We had hoped, ere many years had turned about, to have presented you with a rich and well-peopled kingdom; from whence, now, with myself, I only bring this composure: "Inter victrices Hederam tibi serpere Laurus." *It needeth more than a single denization, being a double stranger. Sprung from the stock of ancient Roma-*

nes, but bred in the New World, of the rudeness whereof it can but participate; especially having wars and tumult to bring it to light instead of the muses."

SAVAGE, THE. By Pomengo, a Head man and Warrior of the Muscogulgee nation. 12mo, pp. 312. $6 00. Phila. 1813.

"This strange book is very original, very wild, and very American. It is a periodical paper, of which the supposed writer is a native American Indian, residing in the city of Philadelphia. "The good people of this republic," it is said, "have long derived amusement from the journals of polished travellers through barbarous nations. Let us for once reverse the picture, and see what entertainment can be drawn from the observations of a savage upon the manners and customs, vices and virtues of those who boast the advantages of refinement and civilization." Such is the design of the book similar in some respects to Goldsmith's Citizen of the World, The Turkish Spy, The Chinese Spy, Persian Letters, Letters of a Hindoo Ragee, &c., &c."

SHECUT, J. L. E. W. Medical and Philosophical Essays containing Topographical Historical, and other Sketches of the City of Charleston; Easay on the prevailing fever of 1817; Essay on Contagions and Infections, and an Essay on Electric Fluid, &c., the whole of which are designed as illustrative of the domestic origin of the yellow fever of Charleston, and as conducing to the formation of a medical history of the State of South Carolina. Royal 8vo. bds. pp. 262. $2 25. Charleston, 1819.

SHEPARD, THOMAS. The Parable of the Ten Virgins opened and applied, being the substance of divers sermons on Matth. 25, 1-13. Folio. pp. 195. $5 00. Cambridge, 1695.

SHEPARD. Tho Parable of the Ten Virgins opened and applied; being the substance of divers sermons on Matth. 25, 1-13. By Jonathan Mitchell and Thos. Shepard. 12mo. pp. 635. $1 50. Boston, 1852.

SHEPARD, THOMAS. Meditations and spiritual Experiences of. 12mo. pp. 82. $3 00. Very rare. Edinburgh, 1749.

SHEPARD, THOMAS. The Sincere Convert: Discovering the small number of True Believers, and the great difficulty of Saving Conversion. Wherein are excellently and plainly opened these choice and divine principles. 18mo. pp. 238. $1 25. London, 1680.

SHEPARD, THOMAS. Thesis Sabbaticæ, or, The Doctrine of the Sabbath, wherein the Sabbaths, I. Morality, II. Change, III. Beginning, IV. Sanctification, are clearly discussed, which were first handled more largely in sundry Sermons in Cambridge in New England, in opening of the fourth commandment. 12mo. pp. 402. $5 00. London, 1655.

SIMCOE, COL. J. G. Military Journal. A History of the Operations of a Partisan Corps, called the Queen's Rangers, commanded by Col. J. G. Simcoe during the war of the American Revolution. Illustrated by ten engraved Plans of Actions, &c, now first published, with a memoir of the Author and other additions. Large paper. small folio. pp. 328. Calf back and corners. $10. N. York, 1844.

SMITH, JOHN. The Generall Historie of Virginia, New England and the Summer Isles, with the names of the Adventurers, Planters and Governours from their first beginning, Anno, 1584, to this present 1626. With the Proceedings of those severall Colonies and the accidents that befell them in all their journeys and discoveries. Also the Maps and descriptions of all those countryes, their commodities, people, government, customes, and religion yet knowne. Divided into sixe bookes. Folio, pp. 148. *Engraved Title and one Map.* $40. London, 1632.

SMITH, JOHN AUGUSTINE. Prelections on some of the most Important Subjects connected with Moral and Physical Science in opposition to Phrenology, Magnetism, Atheism, and the principles advanced by the author of the Vestiges of Creation. 12mo. pp. 405. Portrait. $2 00. New York, 1853.

SMITH, MRS. E. VALE. History of Newburyport from the earliest settlement of the country to the present time; a Biographical Appendix. 8vo. pp. 414. 2 portraits and 1 plate. $2 25. Newburyport, 1854.

SMITH, WILLIAM. The History of the Province of New York, from the first discovery to the year MDCCXXXII. To which is annexed a description of the country, with a short account of the Inhabitants, their trade, religious and political state, and the constitutions of the courts of Justice in that colony. 4to. pp. 264 Plate, a view of Oswego on lake Ontario. $8 00. London, 1757.

SOUTH CAROLINA. Ode to a friend on our leaving together South Carolina. Written in June, 1780. 4to. pp. 15. $2 00. London, 1783.

SPENCER, AMBROSE, Memorials of, Late Chief Justice of the Supreme Court of the State of New York. Consisting of proceedings of public bodies and meetings and of sermons and addresses upon the occasion of his death and in illustration of his life and character. 8vo. pp. 104. Portrait. (*Privately printed.*) $2 00. Albany, 1849.

ST. URSULA'S CONVENT, or the nun of Canada, containing scenes from real life. 2 vols. in 1. 12mo. $2 00. Kingston, Upper Canada, 1824.

The first Novel written and printed in Canada.

STATE RIGHTS CELEBRATION, Proceedings of the, at Charleston, S. C., July 1st, 1830, containing the Speeches of Hon. Wm. Drayton and Hon. R. Y. Hayne, who were the invited guests; also of Langdon Cheeves, James Hamilton, Jr., and Robert J. Turnbull, Esqs., and remarks of his Honor, the Intendant, H. L. Pinckney, to which is added the volunteer Toasts, given on the occasion. 12mo. pp. 56. $2. Charleston, 1830.

STEDMAN, C., The History of the Origin, Progress and Termination of the American War, by. Who served under Sir W. Howe, Sir H. Clinton, and the Marquis Cornwallis. 2 vols. 8vo. pp. 446–528. $6 00. Dublin, 1794.

STONE, WILLIAM L. Matthias and his Impostures; or the Progress of Fanaticism Illustrated in the Extraordinary case of Robert Matthews and some of his forerunners and disciples. 18mo. pp. 347. $1 50. New York, 1835.

Matthias may be called the Petit Mahomet and this book a second Koran. The narrative records the most extraordinary instances of human credulity to be found in any age of the world. The reader can scarcely avoid the conclusion, that the dupes of this imposter must have laboured under a species of insanity before becoming his converts, otherwise we can not see how they could adopt a creed and sanction practices which none, whose understanding is not utterly besotted, could for a moment tolerate................Western Memorabilia.

STONE, WILLIAM S. Maria Monk and the Nunnery of the Hotel Dieu, being an account of a visit to the convents of Montreal, and refutation of the "awful disclosures," audi alteram partem. 8vo. pp. 56. $1 00. New York, 1836.

STONE, WILLIAM L. Uncas and Miantonomoh; a historical discourse delivered at Norwich, Conn., on the 4th day of July, 1842, on the occasion of the erection of a monument to the memory of Uncas, the white man's friend, and first chief of the Mohegans. 18mo. pp. 209. $1 00. New York, 1842.

Col. Stone was at one time (1817 & 18) *the editor of the Albany Gazette, and for a long time afterwards, editor and principal proprietor of the New York Commercial Advertiser. He was universally looked upon as one of the best of the old conservative editors, and his paper for many years had a wide circulation among the sober, staid and peace loving citizens. His opinions, as a general thing, were held in high authority among his readers; he also held great sway among the literati of New York and the neighboring provinces, but in this respect he had a higher reputation perhaps than he deserved, more especially in the department of bibliography, a field in which he was ambitious of being considered very perfect, but his attainments on this subject were quite superficial and inaccurate as could be easily proved from many of the statements he made from time to time through his otherwise meritorious journal. He was author of a number of books on history, biography, romance, and miscellany, some of which still continue to sell, more especially the life of Red Jacket and Brant the Indian chief. For a complete catalogue of his writings, see Gowan's Bibliographical Biography.*
......................Western Memorabilia.

STROUD, GEORGE M. A Sketch of the Laws relating to Slavery in the several States of the United States of America. Second edition with some alterations and considerable additions. 12mo. pp. 300. $2 00. Philadelphia, 1856.

SEYBERT, ADAM. Statistical Annals; embracing views of the population, commerce, navigation, fisheries, public lands, post offices, revenues, mint, military and naval establishments, &c., &c., of the United States of America. Founded on official documents. 4to. pp. 803. Pub. at $15 00—$3 00. Phila., 1818.

TALBOT, MARY ANN. The Life and surprising Adventures of. In the name of John Taylor. A natural daughter of the late Earl Talbot; giving a true account of her singular adventures, the many hardships she endured in a variety of characters for a number of years, both in the land and sea services. Related by herself. 12mo. pp. 60. $3 00. Portrait. London, N. D.

This Amazon in her excursions appears to have visited both Rhode Island and New York. In the former place a young lady fell in love with her and would become her or his wife at all hazards.

TAYLOR, JAMES B. Lives of Virginia Baptist Ministers. 12mo. pp. 492. $1 50. Richmond, 1838.

This book may be styled the Virginia Baptist Biographical Dictionary. It contains not less than 118 *biographies of the ministers of that denomination.*

TAYLOR, JOHN. Tyranny Unmasked. 8vo, pp. 349. $2 50. Washington, 1822.

THERMOMETRICAL NAVIGATION. Being a series of Experiments and Observations, tending to prove, that by ascertaining the Relative Heat of the Sea Water from time to time, the passage of a ship through the Gulf Stream, and from deep water into soundings, may be discovered in time to avoid danger, although (owing to tempestuous weather,) it may be impossible to heave the lead or observe the heavenly bodies. Extracted from the American Philosophical Transactions. Vol. 2 and 3, with additions and Improvements. 8vo. pr. pp. 113. (with map.) $2 00. Philadelphia, 1799.

THOMAS MOORE, ESQ. An attempt to vindicate the American Character, being principally a reply to the intemperate animadversions of *Thomas Moore, Esq., the Irish Poet.* 8vo. pp. 43. $1 25. Philadelphia, 1806.

THOMAS, ISAIAH. The History of Printing in America; with a biography of Printers and an account of newspapers. To which is prefixed a concise view of the discovery and progress of the art in other parts of the world. 2 vols. 8vo. pp. 487 and 576. A beautiful, clean, perfect and very desirable copy. Half bound and cornered in calf. $20 00.

Another copy. 2 vols. 8vo. Sheep. $15 00. Worcester, 1810.

THOMAS, GABRIEL. An Historical and Geographical Account of the Province and Country of Pennsylvania and of West New Jersey, in America; the richness of the soil, the sweetness of the situation, the wholesomeness of the air, the navigable rivers and others, the prodigious increase of corn, &c., &c. 12mo. pp. 100. $1 50. Reprint, New York, 1848. London, 1698.

THOMPSON, CHARLES. The Holy Bible containing the Old and New Covenant, commonly called the Old and New Testament, translated from the Greek. 4 vols. 8vo. Sheep binding. $12 00. Philadelphia, 1808.

Copies of this remarkable version of the Holy Scriptures are now become very scarce. The venerable translator was secretary to the American Congress from 1774 to 1789, and died August 16, 1824.

TRAIN, GEORGE FRANCIS. Young America in Wall Street. 12mo. pp. 406. $1 25. New York, 1857.

TRIBUNE CLUB. The. Proceedings of 1855. Presentation—Anniversary—Dinner. Contains a long poem by Mr. Otterson. 8vo. pp. 32. 50 cts. New York, 1855.

UNITED STATES. A Summary Review of the Laws of the United States of North America, the British Provinces and the West Indias, with observations, precedents, &c. By a barrister of the State of Virginia. 8vo. pp. 103. $1 25. Edinburgh, 1788.

VON STAEHLIN, J. An Account of the New Northern Archipelago, lately discovered by the Russians in the seas of Kamtschatka and Anadir, translated from the German Original, with a colored Map. 8vo. Old calf. pp. 138. $1 00. London, 1774.

WALL STREET, or, Ten Minutes before Three, a Farce in three parts. 18mo. pp. 34, and other pamphlets. $1 50. New York, 1818.

WALL STREET. Stocks and Stock Jobbing in Wall Street, with Sketches of the brokers and fancy stocks. By a Reformed Stock Gambler. 8vo. pp. 40. $2 00. New York, 1848.

WAR, A Complete History of, From the Annual Register, of its Rise, Progress and Events in Europe, Asia, Africa and America. Exhibiting the state of the Belligerent Powers at the commencement of the war; their interests and objects in its continuance; interspersed with the characters of the able and disinterested Statesmen, to whose wisdom and integrity, and of the Heroes, to whose courage and conduct, we are indebted for that naval and military success, which is not to be equalled in the Annals of this or any other nation. 8vo. pp. 627. Plates on a fine view of the town and fortification of Montreal, in Canada. $3 00. Dublin, 1774.

WASHINGTON, GEORGE. Diary of; from the first day of October 1789, to the tenth day of March, 1790, from the original manuscript, now first printed. 8vo. pp. 89. Uncut. $5 00. *Only* 100 *copies printed.* New York, 1858.

WASHINGTON, GEORGE, Life of, by John Marshall (Chief Justice of the United States, 5 vols. 4to. Portrait and Military Plans. $20 00. London, 1804.

The Same Work. 5 vols. 8vo. bds. uncut. A very fine copy. $13 00. London, 1804.

WEBSTER, M. H. A catalogue of the minerals which have been discovered in the State of New York, arranged under the heads of the respective counties and towns in which they are found. 18mo. pp. 32. $1 00. Albany, 1824.

WEBSTER, NOAH. Effects of Slavery on Morals and Industry. 8vo. pp. 56. $1. Hartford, 1793.

WEBSTER, NOAH. A Compendious Dictionary of the English Language. In which five thousand words are added to the number found in the best English compends; the orthography is, in some instances corrected; the pronunciation marked by an accent or other suitable direction; and the definitions of many words amended and improved; to which are added for the benefit of the merchant, the student and the traveller. 12mo. pp. 431. $5 00. Hartford, 1806.

This is the nucleus of the now famous Webster Dictionary. It has become very rare. This copy is in fine, clean and perfect condition.

WHITEFIELD, GEORGE. A Journal of a Voyage from Gibralter to Georgia, containing many curious observations and edifying reflections, on the several occurrences that happened in the voyage. pp. 34. London, 1738.

To which is added a journal of a voyage from London to Savannah, in Georgia. In two parts. Part I. from London to Gibralter. Part II. from Gibralter to Savannah. By George Whitefield. pp. 58. London, 1738.

Also remarks on the Rev. Mr. Whitefield's Journal, wherein his many inconsistencies are pointed out, and his tenets considered. pp. 32. London, N. D.

Twell, on the Demoniacs of the New Testament, proving that they were fallen angels Peculiar Thoughts in the Manner of Mons. Pascal, with divers other curious pamphlets. 8vo. calf. $3 50. London, V. D.

WHITTLESEY, CHARLES. Fugitive Essays upon interesting and useful subjects, relating to the early history of Ohio, its geology and agriculture, with a biography of the first successful constructor of steam; a dissertation upon the antiquity of the material universe, &c., &c. 12mo. pp. 397. $1 25. Hudson, Ohio, 1852.

WILLIAMS, ROGER. A Key into the Language of America, or an help to the language of the natives in that part of America called New England; together with briefe observations of the customes, manners, and worships, &c., of the aforesaid natives in, peace and warre, in life and death. On all which are added, spiritual observations generall and particular, by the author, of chiefe and speciall use (upon all occasions) to all the English inhabiting those parts; yet pleasant and profitable to the view of all men. 8vo. pp. 165. uncut $5 00. London, 1643. reprint. Providence, 1827.

WILLIAMSON, PASSMORE Case of. Report of the proceedings on the writ of Habeas Corpus, issued by Hon. John K. Kane, in the case of the United States of America, ex rel. John H. Wheeler vs. Passmore Williamson, including several opinions delivered, &c. 8vo. pp. 191. $2 00. Philadelphia, 1856.

WILSON, ALEXANDER, American Ornithology, or the Natural History of the Birds of the U. S., illustrated with plates engraved and colored from original drawings taken from Nature. Vols. 2, 3, 4, 5, 6, 7, and 9. 6 vols. folio, with 48 plates. *Original edition.* $25 00. Philadelphia, 1810–14.

WILSON, JAMES. An Introductory Lecture to a Course of Law Lectures. To which is added a plan of the Lectures. 8vo. pr. pp. 96. $1 00. Philadelphia, 1791.

WISCONSIN. First Annual Report and collections of the State Historical Society. of. For the year 1854. 8vo. pp. 160, $1 25. Madison, 1855.

WISE, JOHN. A vindication of the Government of New England Churches. Drawn from antiquity, the light of nature, Holy Scripture, its noble nature, and from the dignity Divine Providence has put upon it. 12mo $3 00 Boston, 1772.

WOLLEY, EDWARD, D. D. Loyalty among Rebels; the True Royalist, or Hushay the Archite, a happy counsellor in King David's greatest danger. To which is added a parallel between Charles II., King of England, and Lewis the IV., the French King. 18mo. pp. 180. $5 50. London, 1662.

WOOLEY, CHARLES. A Two Years Journal in New York; and parts of its Territories in America. By C. W. 18mo. pp. 104. $63 00. London, 1701.

"*This is one of the very scarcest books written in and relating to New York in colonial times. It was produced by the author while a resident on the Island of Manhattan, in the capacity of a chaplain to the troops then occupying the fort situated on the extreme southern point of the Island, known now as the Battery. I have heard of no copy being in the possession of any of the veteran collectors of rare American books on this continent, with the exception of one in the extensive collection of John Carter Brown, Esq., of Providence, Rhode Island.*"

WOOLEY, CHARLES. A Two years Journal in New York; and parts of its Territories in America. A new edition with copious historical and biographical notes by E. B. O'Callaghan, M. D. 8vo. cloth to match Denton's New Netherlands. $2 00. New York, 1860.

WOOLEY, CHARLES. The same as above, large paper. 4to. cloth. Only a few printed. $5 00. New York, 1860.

WRIGHT, FRANCES. (*Mad. D'Arusmont.*) Biography, notes and political letters of *Frances Wright D'Arusmont.* From the first British Edition. 12mo. pp. 48. New York, 1844. Published by John Windt.

ZANGER, JOHN PETER. A brief narrative of the Case and Trial of John P. Zanger, Printer of the New York Weekly Journal for a Libel. 4to. pp. 53. Uncut. $2 00. New York, 1770.

ZARATE, D'AUGUSTIN DE. Histoire de la De Couverte et de la conquete du Perou, illustrated with map and plates. 2 vols. 12mo. calf. pp. 398, 482. $5 00. Paris, 1742.

AMERICAN BIBLIOGRAPHY.

ALIBONE, S. AUSTIN. A Critical Dictionary of English Literature, and British and American Authors, *Living and Deceased*, from the earliest account to the middle of the Nineteenth Century. Containing Thirty Thousand Biographies and Literary Notices, with Forty Indexes of Subjects. 2 vols. Royal 8vo. Pages about 2000. $10. Philadelphia, 1859-60.

BURCH, SAMUEL. General Index to the Laws of the United States of America, from March 4th, 1789 to March 3d, 1827. Including all Treaties entered into between those periods. 8vo. pp. 331. $2 00. Washington, 1828.

CHARACTER *of Law Books and Judges* With Remarks on the Utility of Collecting. 8vo. pp. 66. See The American Jurist, July, 1834. Boston, 1334.

DECANVER, H. C. *Pseud.* Catalogue of Works in Refutation of Methodism, from its origin in 1729, to the present time; of those by Methodist authors on lay representation, Methodist episcopacy, etc., etc., and of the political pamphlets relating to Wesley's "Calm Address to the American Colonies:" (C. H. Cavender). 8vo. pp. 54. Philadelphia, 1846.

DICKINS' ASBURY. A Synoptical Index to the Laws and Treaties of the United States of America, from March 4, 1789, to March 3, 1851. With references to the Edition of the Laws Published by Bioren and Duane, and of the Statutes at Large, Published by Little and Brown, under the Authority of Congress. Royal 8vo. pp. 747. $5 00. Boston, 1856.

GENERAL INDEX To the Laws of the State of New York, from 1777 to 1850. 8vo. pp. 665. $2 00. Law binding. New York, 1850.

GOWANS, WILLIAM. American Bibliographical Biography. Being a Catalogue of all the Books written by American Authors, or those who have resided in America, with their size, number of pages, if illustrated by engravings or maps, when and where printed; with a short biographical sketch of each author. 6 vol. 4to. (In manuscript.) New York, N. D.

GOWANS, WILLIAM. A Catalogue of all the books known to have been written on *Pastoral Care and Ministerial Duties.* 12mo. (In manuscript.) New York.

GOWANS, WILLIAM. A Catalogue of Books on Freemasonry and Kindred Subjects. 12mo. pp. 59. $1 25. New York, 1858.

GOWANS, WILLIAM. A Catalogue of all the books known to have been written on the History, Culture, Use, Abuse and Influence of *Tobacco*, from its discovery, by Europeans, to the present time. 12mo. (In manuscript.) New York, N. D.

GOWANS, WILLIAM. A Catalogue of all the books known to have been written on the *Theory and Practice of Dancing.* (In manuscript.) New York, N. D.

GOWANS, WILLIAM. A Catalogue of Books of Proverbs, Sayings, Maxims, Apophthegms, Adages and Similitudes. By Ancients, Intermediates and Moderns. 12mo. pp. 16. New York, 1853.

GOWANS, WILLIAM. A Catalogue of all the Books by various authors on the subject of the *Immortality of the Soul.* 12mo. pp. 22. New York, 1853.

GOWANS, WILLIAM. A Catalogue of the Scottish Poets and Poetry. 12mo. pp. 24. New York, 1852.

GOWANS, WILLIAM. A Catalogue of Books on the Evidence of Revealed Religion. By the most Eminent Authors. 12mo. pp. 30. New York, 1853.

GUILD, REUBEN A. The Librarian's Manual; A Treatise on Bibliography. comprising a select and descriptive list of Bibliographical Works; to which are added Sketches of Public Libraries, Illustrated with Engravings. 4to. pp. 314. $5. New York, 1858.

HAYNES, THOMAS WILSON. Baptist Cyclopædia; or Dictionary of Baptist Biography, Bibliography, Antiquities, History, Chronology, Theology, Poetry and Literature; to which is added a list of the Baptist Churches in England and America. 3 Portraits. Royal 8vo. pp. 323. vol. I all published. $1 50. Charleston, S. C., 1848.

JEWETT, CHARLES C. Notices of Public Libraries in the United States of America. Being an Appendix to the Fourth of the Smithsonian Institution. 8vo. pp. 207. Washington, 1851.

LA ROCHE, R., M. D Bibliography of Yellow Fever. 8vo. pp. 60. Philadelphia, 1855.

This bibliography was prepared as a pendant to the author's celebrated treatise on Yellow Fever. He had intended to have had a small edition printed separately at the same time that the treatise was printed, but unfortunately, before he had informed the printer of his intentions, the type had gone into pi, thereby verifying the old adage "for want of a nail, the horse was lost."

LIST OF MAPS and Memoirs on the Geology of North America, forming part of Jules Marcou's Geology of North America. 4to. pp. 22. Zurich, 1858.

LUDEWIG, HERMANN E. The Literature of American Local History; a Bibliographical Essay. 8vo. pp. 180. $6 00.

This book possesses very considerable merit, as well for its accuracy as for its intrinsic worth as an Index to American Local History. The diligent and conscientious author copied every title from the respective books themselves, and not from catalogues, as is too frequently the case in making such compilation, except in a few cases where he had titles sent to him by his book-loving friends throughout the states, whose accuracy and taste he could depend upon. It is the first and so far the only bibliography of the kind, relating to this subject. It was privately printed, and immediately on its appearance, distributed by its generous author among his friends in America and Europe.

He had contemplated a second and enlarged edition, and, indeed, had made considerable progress in collecting material for that purpose, when, alas, alas, the grim messenger put a sudden stop to his noble enterprise, an event, the knowledge of which, filled every one who had the happiness to know him, with deep regret at losing such a valuable member of society.—Western Memorabilia.

LUDEWIG, HERMANN E. The Literature of American Aboriginal Languages, with Additions and Corrections by William W. Turner. Edited by Nicholas Trübner. 8vo. pp. 283. $3 00. London, 1858.

MARVIN J. G. Legal Bibliography; or a Thesaurus of American, English, Irish and Scotch law books, together with some continental treatises; interspersed with some critical observations upon their various editions and authority. To which is added a copious list of abbreviations. 8vo. pp. 800. $6 50. Philadelphia, 1847.

NEW YORK STATE LIBRARY. Catalogue of the Books on Bibliography and Engravings in the New York State Library. 8vo. pp. 143. Albany, 1858.

NORTON, CHARLES B. Literary Register, or Annual Book List for 1856. A Catalogue of Books, including New Editions and Reprints published in the United States, during the year 1855. Containing Titles, Number of Pages, Prices and Name of Publishers, with an Index of the Subjects. 8vo. pp. 138. New York, 1856.

This was originally intended to be an annual publication.

O'CALLAGHAN, E. B. A list of various editions of the Holy Scriptures, and parts thereof, printed in the United States previous to 1860: to which is appended a list of the earlier American editions of the Psalms in Metre, with an introduction and bibliographical notes, by E. B. O'Callaghan. Royal 8vo. Albany, 1860.

POOLE, WILLIAM FRED. An Index to Periodical Literature. Royal 8vo. pp. 533. $2 50. Published at $7 00. New York, 1853.

The above is a very full and carefully prepared index of all the subjects treated of in not less than seventy-three of the most popular periodicals published during the present century, in Great Britain and the United States of North America. It will be found to be an immense labor-saving machine to any person having cause to investigate these store-houses of intellectual riches; the product of the most gifted minds that have appeared on the stage of human action and mental effort, during the last sixty years.

PRINCE, BENJAMIN. A Catalogue of Works Relating to *Sound*, Arranged Chronologically under each subject. 8vo. pp. 56. Boston, 1836.

This bibliograhy is made a pendant to the author's treatise on sound, never having appeared otherwise.

PURPLE, SAMUEL, M. D. Bibliotheca Medica. A Bibliographical Account of the Medical Periodical Literature of the United States. 8vo. (In manuscript.) New York, 1860.

RHEES, WILLIAM I. Manual of Public Libraries, Institutions and Societies in the United States, and British Provinces of North America. 8vo. pp. 715. $4. Phila., 1859.

REES, JAMES. The Dramatic Authors of America. 12mo. pp. 144. $1. Phila., 1845.

ROORBACH, O. A. Bibliotheca Americana. Catalogue of American Publications, including Reprints and original Works from 1820 to 1852, inclusive, together with a list of Periodicals Published in the United States. 8vo. pp. 673. $5. New York, 1852.

ROORBACH, O. A. Supplement to the Bibliotheca Americana. A Catalogue of American Publications, Reprints and Original Works, from October, 1852, to May, 1855. Including, also, a repetition of such books as have either changed prices or publishers during that period. 8vo. pp. 227. $3 00. New York, 1855.

SHEA, JOHN GILMARY. A Bibliographical Account of Catholic Bibles, Testaments and other portions of the Scriptures, Translated from the Latin Vulgate, and printed in the United States. 12mo. pp. 48. $1 25. New York, 1859.

The first bibliography of the kind published in the United States of North America.

WILLES, WILLIAM. A Descriptive Catalogue of Books and Pamphlets Relating to the State of Maine, or portions of it. pp. 20. Small 4to. New York, 1859.

C. B. Norton intends to publish, in future Nos. of his Literary Letter, the Bibliography of each separate State.

www.ingramcontent.com/pod-product-compliance
Lightning Source LLC
LaVergne TN
LVHW021425110826
845150LV00007B/2081